HOMEGROWN
MARIJUANA

CREATE A **HYDROPONIC GROWING SYSTEM**
IN YOUR OWN HOME

JOSHUA SHEETS

COOL SPRINGS PRESS

Home and Garden Experts™

MINNEAPOLIS, MINNESOTA

First published in 2015 by Cool Springs Press, an imprint of Quarto Publishing Group USA Inc.,
400 First Avenue North, Suite 400, Minneapolis, MN 55401 USA

© 2015 Quarto Publishing Group USA Inc.

Text © 2015 Joshua Sheets

The information in this book is true and complete to the best of our knowledge. All
recommendations are made without any guarantee on the part of the author or Publisher,
who also disclaims any liability incurred in connection with the use of this data or specific details.

We recognize, further, that some words, model names, and designations mentioned herein are
the property of the trademark holder. We use them for identification purposes only. This is not
an official publication.

Cool Springs Press titles are also available at discounts in bulk quantity for industrial or sales-
promotional use. For details write to Special Sales Manager at Quarto Publishing Group USA Inc.,
400 First Avenue North, Suite 400, Minneapolis, MN 55401 USA.

To find out more about our books, visit us online at www.coolspringspress.com.

Library of Congress Cataloging-in-Publication Data
Sheets, Joshua, 1981- author.
 Homegrown marijuana : create a hydroponic growing system in your own home / Joshua Sheets.
    pages cm
 Includes index.
 ISBN 978-1-59186-910-8 (sc)
 1. Cannabis. 2. Marijuana. 3. Hydroponics. I. Title.

SB295.C35S48 2015
633.7'9--dc23
                                          2015012204

Acquisitions Editor: Billie Brownell
Project Manager: Jordan Wiklund
Art Director: Cindy Samargia Laun
Book Design: Laurie Young
Photography: John Barber, Rau+Barber
Illustration: Shannon Rahkola

Printed in China

10 9 8 7 6 5 4 3 2 1

Dedication and Acknowledgments

I would like to thank my family for sticking with me as I gained the knowledge and experience necessary to write this book. And to my partner in crime, James Durham, for being my best and brightest pupil, as well as my best friend, thank you. Thanks to Drew Kepner and to the Rexious family, particularly Kern Rexious. Thanks to Ed Ansorg and Vicki Buckman from Peninsula College. And to many others: Diane and Paul Williamson, the original small town crew, Jared from Rainier Acres, Mike Flieshman and Mike Tullis, Jack Herer, Jeremy Garretson, Lyle Bing, Christopher Estes, D' Haney King, Joe Fry, Todd Blogette, Josh Ramsey, Angelo Lumbardini, Armando Reed, and Carl and Connie Durham. And last, an acknowledgment of all the guys locked up in Washington DOC for cannabis-related charges and all the inmates participating in the horticulture program.

This book is dedicated to everyone, anywhere, who grows cannabis to treat themselves, grows it to help people, or any combination of the two.

Contents

CHAPTER 1

Getting Started on a Home-Based System

The story of cannabis is practically as old as modern culture. It was described in a Chinese medical compendium considered to date from 2737 BC. Its use spread from China to India and then to North Africa and reached Europe at least as early as AD 500. A major crop in colonial North America, cannabis (hemp) was grown as a source of fiber. Hemp has made a comeback as an agricultural crop, with nearly $500 million in retail sales of hemp products in the United States in 2012.

Its use as an intoxicant was also commonplace from the 1850s to the 1930s. A campaign conducted in the 1930s by the United States Federal Bureau of Narcotics sought to portray marijuana as a powerful, addictive substance that would lead users into narcotics addiction. In the 1950s it was an accessory of the Beat Generation; in the 1960s it was used by college students and "hippies" and became a symbol of rebellion against authority. However, medicinally it was and is prescribed for various conditions including labor pains, nausea, and rheumatism.

The Controlled Substances Act of 1970 classified marijuana, along with heroin and LSD, as a Schedule I drug. Most marijuana at that time came from Mexico, but in 1975 the Mexican government agreed to eradicate the Mexican crop by spraying it with the herbicide paraquat, raising fears of toxic side effects. Colombia then became the main supplier.

The "zero tolerance" climate of the Reagan and Bush administrations (1981–1993) resulted in passage of strict laws and mandatory sentences for possession of marijuana as well as in heightened vigilance against smuggling at the southern borders. The "War on Drugs" brought with it a shift from reliance on

Opposite: If you plan to grow more than one or two plants at home, it usually makes the most sense to construct a self-contained grow room where you can control the growing environment precisely.

My Story

When I was thirteen, I began having symptoms of a rare neurological disorder. After two years of being misdiagnosed repeatedly, and trying a ton of prescription drugs, I was ready to try any cure. During this period I was also a rebellious youth, as many are, and I tried smoking marijuana. I noticed an increase in the duration between episodes. The prescription drugs were expensive, they weren't working, and they had awful side effects. If medical marijuana had been approved in my state, that would have been the end of the story (assuming I could have found an ample supply that was both affordable and powerful and the purveyor would sell to a fifteen-year-old). But that wasn't the case, so I took my limited knowledge of gardening and I germinated seeds I found in bags in order to grow my own cure.

My first crop took heavy losses from a local herd of deer, but I was hooked on the thrill of having the power to treat myself. The need for relief in the winter months drove me indoors; there, the botany bug really bit me. Some might say my lust for the best flower ran hand in hand with greed, but I think back on those years as something purer. Then I was arrested and sent to prison, unfortunately.

During incarceration I was given the opportunity to attend college. After graduating with a 3.98 GPA, I combined my knowledge and experience into a position as a teacher's aide. Obvious holes in a hydroponics curriculum gave me a desire to write text to fill in the syllabus. That was the basis for this book.

When recreational marijuana was legalized in my state (Washington), I was in a prison work-release facility working as a nurseryman. Because of frequent pain from my condition, I procured a medical marijuana recommendation the day I was released from probation. It's an incredible coincidence and irony to be released from prison for a crime a few weeks after that crime is legalized. I'm not the type to look a gift horse in the mouth, and Seattle was in need of experienced horticulturists.

Now I live in a beautiful valley in the Puget Sound, quietly managing a nursery and helping local gardeners (of all kinds) with their needs. Currently I'm setting my own personal record for longest gap between neurological episodes by treating myself with medical marijuana.

—Joshua Sheets

imported supplies to domestic cultivation (particularly in Hawaii and California). Beginning in 1982, the Drug Enforcement Administration (DEA) increased attention to marijuana farms in the United States, and there was a shift toward the indoor growing of plants specially developed for small size and high yield.

After more than a decade of decreasing use, marijuana smoking began an upward trend once more in the early 1990s, but by the end of the decade this upswing had leveled off well below former peaks of use. California legalized medicinal marijuana with the passage of Proposition 215 in the mid-'90s, followed by Washington and other states. In 2012, Washington and Colorado legalized separate systems for medical and recreational use. Internationally, Spain and a handful of other countries have taken a tolerant stance toward legal cannabis consumption. This link has a chart of marijuana legislation: www.ncsl.org/research/health/state-medical-marijuana-laws.aspx.

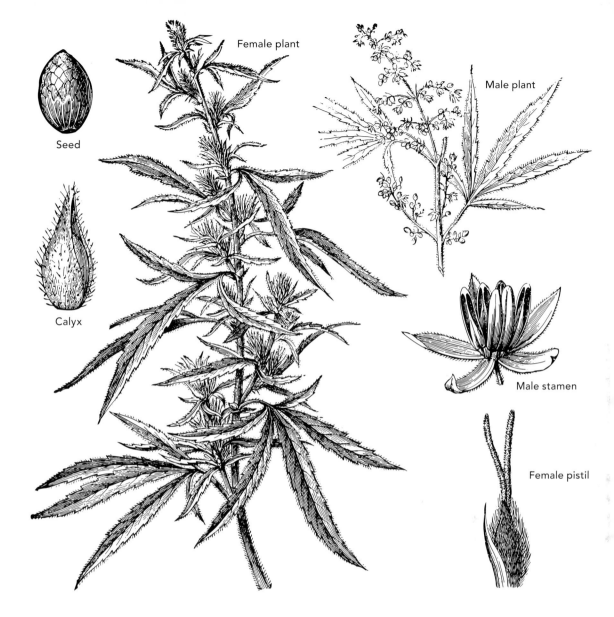

Seed

Calyx

Female plant

Male plant

Male stamen

Female pistil

CANNABIS PLANT ORIGINS

The cannabis plant is theorized to have its origins rooted in central Asia during the Pleistocene glaciations about 1,800 years ago. Based on pollen count reconstructions, this is believed to have been a cold, dry period in Earth's history. Stemming from this period are four distinct varieties in widespread cultivation: *Cannabis sativa*, *Cannabis indica*, *Cannabis ruderalis* and *Cannabis afghanica*.

Cannabis sativa is believed to have sprouted in the Black Sea region, possibly in the Caucasus Mountains, and stretching down to the sea in a warm, often lush, environment. It is a plant that exhibits greater vertical height, longer flowering times, and distinct terpenoid (active chemical) combinations. *Cannabis sativa* and its hybrids have many desirable traits, including distinct flavors and cannabinoid combinations, large vertical height, and strong resistance to diseases and pests in environments ranging from temperate to tropical. Its

Marijuana plants are either male or female: you need both for pollination to occur. Clockwise from the top left are the seed, female plant, male plant, male stamen, female pistil, and calyx.

This is a typical *Cannabis indica* growth structure.

growth structure is characterized by long internodal spacing (a big space between leaves on the stem). Prolific growth during vegetation is common, and leaves are typically characterized by distinctly long leaflets (fingers) that do not overlap (palm-shaped leaves). When grown outdoors in temperate environments, *C. sativa* tends to be much taller, is darker green, and has long, thin buds of unusual structures and/or colors with distinct flavors. Many of the heirloom varieties take up to 14-plus weeks to flower in temperate environments outside. This has led to *C. sativa*'s availability becoming limited. Varieties traded and sold as *C. sativa* are actually often-mislabeled hybrids whose selected phenotype displays some or all of the structural characteristics but that have more desirable flowering times and that yield a higher final weight. More reputable merchants have taken to labeling hybrids as "sativa dominant" to avoid misleading their clientele. Botanists have begun referring to these varieties as NLD, or narrow leaf drug plants.

Cannabis indica is believed to have sprouted in China in what is the modern-day Hung Duong province. While China was warmer than areas to the north twelve thousand years ago, it was probably not an ideal environment. Generally, elevations in Hung Duong province are higher with thinner air, a glaring sun, and pest problems that are of a very different sort than those found around the Black Sea. *C. indica* plants tend to have shorter profiles and flowering times. Wider flowers that possess larger amounts of THC (Tetrahydrocannabinol, the desirable active ingredient in cannabis that is ingested) are common, leading to this variety spreading all over the earth thanks to man. The terpenoid range of these varieties is diverse but also very different from *C. sativa*. When grown outdoors in temperate environments, *C. indica* will be much shorter than *C. sativa*. Its leaves can range in color from lime green to very dark green. Its leaflets are wide and often much shorter than *C. sativa* or hybrids. Botanists have also begun referring to these varieties as WLD, or wide leaf drug plants.

It is impossible to know for sure exactly what happened thousands of years ago. The current theories provide lots of research-based insight into what *could* have taken place and certainly illustrate the difficulty of classifying a plant as diverse as cannabis. Calling a piece of dried flower *sativa-* or *indica*-dominant is used when marketing the finished product and is really just being used as a tool to describe the aftereffects of ingestion. It does not necessarily indicate the true genetics of the plant.

Plants that produce complex psychoactive compounds while flowering often produce a wide range of effects. In cannabis, the state of maturity of the capitate trichome at harvest strongly influences whether the cannabis ingested

Cannabis plants typically mature in distinct stages. This sequence shows *Cannabis indica* in three stages of vegetation.

causes feelings of euphoria versus a generally sedative effect. Both can be disorienting in a high dose. Generally, the rule of thumb is that if the capitate trichome, a mushroom-like, hair-like structure on the surface of a leaf or flower (see page 18), is clear to cloudy, the finished product will produce a less sedative effect when ingested. The more it matures from cloudy to amber, the more the finished product will produce a sedative effect when ingested.

Most cannabis hybrids are combinations of plants from these two gene pools. This has led to abundant diversity in size, structure, color, potency, and secondary chemical compositions. Most breeding has been concerned with increasing the potency of cannabinoids by hybridization and selection for flavor compounds or for desirable coloration.

Today hybridizers are breeding out the photoperiodic triggers in cultivars commonly grown for consumption. When bred with a variety of cannabis commonly referred to as **C. ruderalis**, found to be a nonphotoperiodic or autoflowering plant, and then selectively rebred, popular varieties become more container friendly without the need for artificial night (dark period) during flowering. This greatly aids efficiency for assembly line or cyclical production processes, but the tradeoff is usually a lower cannabinoid content.

Other noted varieties of cannabis exist such as **C. afghanica**, a WLD subset cultivated for the production of hashish in a high-altitude, high-heat environment with substantial pests. Selection and environmental conditions have led to leaf and stem growth structures and cannabinoid combinations not displayed in other *Cannabis* varieties. *C. afghanica* varieties are typically wide in leaf and thick in the stem formation, sometimes displaying a pronounced throat

vein. Its leaflets are wide to thin but overlap where they meet. Some leaf formations in *C. afghanica* can appear twisted or deep veined, and as such may give the appearance of early onset of potassium or trace element deficiencies. The leaves are lighter in coloration, in general, while flowering with extreme pubescence (hairy texture) and a noticeably rich flavor.

The cannabis seed industry has taken to conducting safari-type cultivations of drug varieties in reaches near and far. Most are cataloged, stored, and released as originals after some production and then bred with other cultivars to blend desirable characteristics. While the amount of diversity in currently circulated strains is staggering, they are susceptible to homogenization like *C. afghanica*. Heirloom varieties can be very different when compared to current cultivars.

A young Cannabis indica plant in a pre-flowering stage.

GETTING STARTED

Growing your own marijuana hydroponically is completely within reach of anyone with the space, time, and attention to detail. While it isn't necessarily complicated to set up a system, all hydroponic systems have a lot of variables, and you need to have a basic understanding of those variables before you can decide which system is best for you.

This book goes through each of the elements of a hydroponic system for marijuana. It then discusses pests and troubleshooting, harvesting, and ingesting.

COMPONENTS OF A HOME-BASED HYDROPONIC SYSTEM

In order to build an organized system that delivers the results you're looking for, you need to have a good understanding of the main components of a hydroponic system.

Space

You can set up a hydroponic marijuana system in an area as small as a closet or as large as a garage. The larger the environment and the more plants growing, the more concerns you'll have keeping everything healthy. It's important to know that everything with marijuana production is scalable.

There are two aspects of space to sort out:

- **Where you grow the plants:** The *grow room* is a larger overall room where the growing environment is located. The *growing environment* is a smaller closet or setup with lights, a watering system, and so forth. They are two separate things.

- **Electrical requirements:** The fans, lights, pumps, and all of the other equipment necessary to set up a system take a lot of power. It is possible that you will have to upgrade the electrical capabilities within the grow room so that you can operate the growing environment.

Equipment

Once you have your growing space sorted out, you will use equipment to build the growing environment. Growing environments are built from the following types of equipment or components:

- **Lights:** Marijuana plants are photosensitive, meaning they are triggered into bloom (producing the part of the plant that you harvest for use) based on the number of hours of daylight and darkness. In order to get the plants to bloom, you have to have lights.
- **Circulation:** Fans and CO_2 systems keep the plants from overheating and ensure enough "raw materials" for plants to work with to photosynthesize (meaning, to produce carbohydrates via photosynthesis).
- **Growing media:** This is the material in which you "plant" the plants. These are all soilless. Growing media is primarily to support the plants physically, not to give them any sort of sustenance.
- **Watering systems:** This is the meat and potatoes of hydroponics. These are the systems where you plant and grow the plants, through which you run the nutrient solution that feeds and waters the plants. The type of watering system you use depends on the number of plants you are growing and at what stage of growth the plants are in.

Cannabis indica vegetates in a drip bucket system.

Put these components together and you can build a hydroponic system within the growing environment within the grow room. Whether you are growing one plant or one hundred, there is a system setup that will work for you.

Nutrient Solutions

The nutrient solution is the way you deliver water and nutrients to your plants. The solution will differ depending on the stage of growth of the plants. You can buy premixed nutrient solutions and/or mix and tweak your own.

Putting It All Together

All of these together add up to create a home-based hydroponic system for growing your own marijuana.

CHAPTER 2

Growing Marijuana

Before you can start planning production techniques or watering systems, you first need to understand how a marijuana plant grows. It's important to know what's available—in terms of plant material. Then, once you've secured the plants or seeds, you need to know the parts of the plant—so you know where to prune, how to manipulate the plant to produce a harvest, and what to harvest.

Once you learn the parts of the plant, get to know the cannabis plant life cycle—the changes that the plants naturally undergo as they grow and changes that you can make to the plants' environment that can facilitate certain reactions within the plants.

Above: This is what healthy and viable cannabis seeds look like.

Opposite: Marijuana plants require large amounts of light often on a 24-hour-per-day basis.

TYPES OF CANNABIS PLANTS

When deciding on cultivars to grow, there are a few things to consider. Eventual mature size is a good starting point. Taller plants can be cumbersome in smaller gardens, and shorter plants can be disappointing in larger, more spacious setups. Consider the size of your garden. If you're growing for potency, find a variety known for the strength of the THC compound. If you're growing for a special flavor or appearance, select varieties you have tried as a final product, or ones close to it. Use the Internet sites from states where growing is legal or from abroad to compare what you think you have to what you want. Take anything on the Internet with a grain of salt.

Acquiring plants or seeds can be one of the most challenging aspects of growing cannabis. Be extra careful ordering seeds over the Internet; it can

be risky. Accepting clones from other gardeners can, and often will, contaminate your garden with their pests or fungi. Plants from dispensaries, farmers markets, and Internet sites can be as rife with pests and disease as those from a box store or old, dirty nursery. Always quarantine plants received from these sources for a couple of weeks while you observe their growth.

An alternative to using cuttings, transplants, or seed purchased somewhere is to use seed found in dried flowers. Called bag seed, this is often an S-type seed or, if you're lucky, an F1 hybrid. If it's an S-type seed produced from common environmental problems in improper gardens, it will be very similar to what you found it in. F1 hybrids are only common in product from mixed cultivar outdoor gardens that aren't visited frequently during early flowering. These seeds could be anything from great to dismal, but they do not contain pests. They also display hybrid vigor and tend to be larger overall and grow faster and are more resistant to pests and disease.

Selecting a plant that will have a tall height at maturity for a small garden isn't the only pitfall to avoid. Due to sloppy production and cultivation, many pests are much more resistant to countermeasures. New pests enter areas from year to year, such as the sugar beet aphid or root aphid, or unfamiliar forms of whiteflies, thrips, gnats, and so forth. At this point, you can't necessarily select for pest resistance based on cultivar. In states where it's legal to grow marijuana, people have started rebreeding proven varieties when they can get their hands on the parent plants to reintroduce popular characteristics. This, however, can yield results that are questionable. You're just going to have to work with your plants over time to see what performs the best.

The variety called 'White Widow' shows extreme diversity in characteristics, while 'Blue Dream' is very much uniform; both are commonly rebred. Some of these rebred varieties display a susceptibility to diseases not commonly associated with cannabis cultivation, such as root rot, calcium or magnesium deficiencies, phosphorus deficiencies, and so forth. This, along with marketing hype, makes sourcing seed from legal markets almost as unreliable as sourcing from illegal ones. The international seed houses that sell their wares as novelty items are reputable as far as labeling cultivars, but naming may differ from company to company. If you're living and growing in a place where cannabis has just been made legal, bag seed might be your best option.

If you end up growing a variety that you don't necessarily like, it may be advantageous for you to attempt to breed it with the next variety you get (to create a cross). Using stress or hormones to induce a female plant to produce pollen and fertilize a second female plant can yield enough seed disparity (differences in the plants that grow from the seeds resulting from the cross) to give you a shot at a set of more desirable characteristics. The increase in vigor should be present to a good degree even if the plants grown from seed are similar to the parents. Continued back breeding may be necessary in a situation where no other cultivars are readily attainable to achieve a plant with the

most desirable characteristics. When you're making choices about breeding, always keep your original intent in mind. Don't select a plant displaying squatty characteristics from one lot and then select a tall plant from the next lot unless that tall plant has a very noticeable improvement in another characteristic that can't be overlooked, such as exceptional coloration or potency.

Whiteflies (left) and fungus gnats (right) are common pests for the home marijuana grower.

PARTS OF A CANNABIS PLANT

Cannabis plants are *dioecious* flowering plants, which means there are male and female plants (the male and female flowers are on different plants). The part of the plant that you will harvest for use is the *female flower*. You might think that you would only want to grow female plants. However, if you want to breed your own varieties, you will have to keep a few male plants around for cross-pollination.

When you obtain cuttings of plants to grow, they will have already been "sexed" (the sex of the plant determined). When you grow plants from seed, you'll have to wait until the plants reach the flowering stage to determine their sex.

These are not the only parts of the plant, but they are the parts of the plant that will be most relevant to you, as a grower.

Fan leaves: Large, palmate-shaped leaves that are the most recognizable part of the cannabis plant (after the flower buds). These leaves are where most photosynthesis takes place.

Sugar leaves: Leaves that grow within the female flowers are known as sugar leaves. They have a high concentration of trichomes and are often curled in shape.

Mature flower bud (female): The top part of the plant that is harvested.

Male flower: Male flowers provide pollen for hybridizing.

Trichomes: Trichomes are hairs on plant leaves. On a cannabis plant, these hairs contain oils with the active ingredient desired by growers.

PARTS OF A PLANT

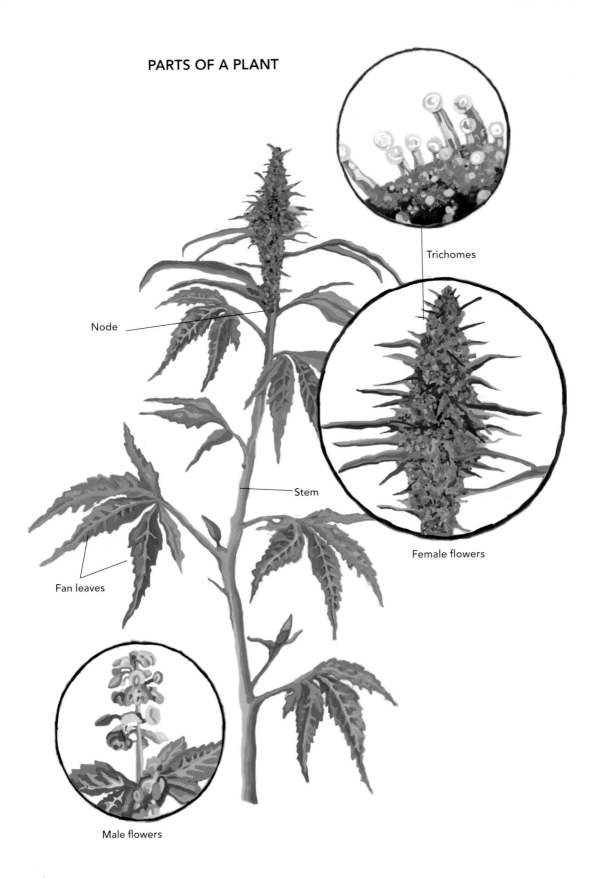

Trichomes

Node

Stem

Female flowers

Fan leaves

Male flowers

Node: The node is the part of the stem from which buds and branches grow.

Internode: The part of the stem between the nodes. Nothing will sprout from the internode.

Root: The part of the plant that takes up water (or the nutrient solution).

Root hairs: These are fine outgrowths of the root that absorb the majority of water, nutrients, and oxygen.

Apical meristem/terminal bud (growing tip): The top of the plant where vertical growth originates.

Pistil: The female reproductive part is the pistil. The pistils are the hairy-looking parts of the female flower buds.

Knowing the parts of a marijuana plant will help you follow the instructions for plant care.

As cannabis finishes flowering, the trichomes, calyxes, and pistil hairs change color.

LIFE CYCLE

Cannabis plants are annual flowering plants. "Annuals," as these types of plants are called, germinate (sprout) from a seed, grow, flower, produce seeds, and die within one year or growth cycle. Some annual plants are stimulated to flower based on day length (light hours vs. dark hours), while others are affected by temperature. Some grow to a certain size or height and then start flowering.

Cannabis plants are photosensitive, which means that you can manipulate lighting to keep the plant in a vegetative (nonflowering) state or move it into a flowering state. Whether you want the plants to be vegetative or flowering depends on what you're doing with the plants at the time: growing for harvest (flowering) or growing to produce cuttings (vegetative).

If you develop your own hybrid varieties, you will perpetuate the plants by growing a mother plant from which you can take cuttings. To grow those cuttings to harvest, you skip the germination stage. Once the cuttings are rooted, they can be treated the same as plants in the second stage of vegetative growth.

Cannabis plants require different conditions and care depending on the stage of growth they're in. Lighting conditions and nutrient solution content are what change the most as the plants grow. Learning about plant growth stages will help you give your plants better care so that you can grow a bigger harvest.

PLANT GROWTH STAGES
Germination

Germination is the process of activating a dormant seed and growing it into a seedling. Seeds need oxygen, the appropriate temperature, and water to germinate successfully. The optimum temperature range for germination is between 75°F to 90°F, but most seeds germinate best at around 86°F with high humidity.

Parts of a Seed

Radicle: Embryonic root

Cotyledon: Seed leaves

Endosperm: Food for the embryonic plant. The plant will use the sugars and starches in the endosperm to grow until it can photosynthesize.

Seed coat: Protective outer coat of the seed. Must be broken in order for the plant to germinate.

Starting Seeds

If you germinate seeds before planting them in your system, you should only plant viable (alive) seeds. (Planting live seeds will save time and money in the long run. You won't waste space on seeds that won't grow.)

GERMINATING IN A PAPER TOWEL

You can germinate seeds in a paper towel. Place seeds between two paper towels and periodically spray with water to keep the towels moist. Gently remove seeds soon after the radicle (embryonic root) pushes itself out in search of growing medium, and place the seeds into a plug, mat, or directly into the desired medium. (The seeds are tiny. You might want to use tweezers.)

A wet paper towel is a good host for getting seeds to germinate.

The paper towel technique has the advantage of allowing you to see which seeds germinate so you can then plant only the viable seeds, but it can be difficult to keep the paper towel at the ideal saturation rate and temperature. An alternative is to use propagation trays and domes to create a closed environment that will provide seeds with the environmental conditions they need to successfully germinate. Use one of the propagation mediums in the form of a mat or plugs. These mats and plugs have small holes already centrally located in the individual squares or plugs to help you site in the seeds.

CANNABIS LIFE CYCLE

1. The cloning stage This stage consists of cutting a branch off an existing female plant and then planting it in a propagation block for seven to 12 days, during which it will grow its own set of roots.

2. The "veg" stage This lasts for approximately two months, during which the plants are subject to light 24 hours a day.

3. The flowering stage The flowering stage takes 50 to 75 days. During this time, the plants are switched to a 12-hour light schedule (12 on, 12 off) using sodium lights, which mimic the fall sunlight.

4. The processing stage During this stage, the plants are cut at the base, hung upside-down, and stripped of their usable parts—the buds, sugar leaves, and so forth.

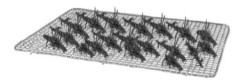

5. The curing stage The curing stage lasts for 2 weeks and consists of drying the buds on screens.

GERMINATING IN A PROPAGATION DOME

1. Prepare a tray with the growing medium (mat or plugs).
2. Place the seeds in the holes already centrally located in the mat or plug, and rip small chunks off the sides of the pieces of medium to plug up the holes.
3. Water the medium so it is *moist*, and spray the inside of the dome with water until it is covered with small droplets. Use tap water that has been sterilized with a UV light. (See pages 41 and 42.)
4. Fit the dome securely on the tray and place it in the reproductive chamber. (See Chapter 6.)
5. Check the seeds in the dome every other day, always making sure that the medium is moist. If you used a propagation tray with inserts, fill the bottom of the tray with just enough water to submerge the bottom centimeter of the medium. The capillary effect will cause the medium to stay moist.
6. Always spray the inside of the dome with a mist of water before leaving. This will ensure high humidity until you come back to check the seedlings.

STAGES OF VEGETATIVE (PLANT) GROWTH
First and Second Stages

The first stage of vegetative growth is the **seedling stage**. The plant remains in this stage from the time the cotyledons push out of the growing medium into the air to the time the second set of true leaves are formed. Because a marijuana plant is so fragile at this point, be careful when transplanting and do not feed them any fertilizer or nutrient solution. Plants at this stage are still using the endosperm (nutrition from the seed) for their nutrient requirements, so clean, tepid water is sufficient.

Within 14 days, most plants will move out of this stage and into the second stage of vegetative growth. Watch the plant for signs of stress, including leaf curl and stretching. If curl is happening, it is most likely stress caused by a problem with the growing medium, which is the catchall term used to describe a problem in the root zone. Check the pH of the water, the temperature of the water, and the moisture level of the medium to make sure it isn't too wet or too dry; these are the most likely culprits. If you identify a problem (pH is off, for example), correct it quickly, and plants will make a full recovery.

Leaf discoloration at this stage is a sign that the endosperm is depleted and the seedling is ready for a very mild nutrient solution. Feed the plant an application of a grow solution at half strength. Nutrient sinks (where stored nutrients) are young and underdeveloped so feeding starches, carbohydrates, and minerals is not necessary, but feeding vitamins and hormones will speed recovery and they will be stored for later use.

These plants are in the first stage of vegetative growth: the seedling stage.

Stretching is elongation of internodal spacing, and is a result of the plant releasing/producing the hormone *gibberellin* in an attempt to find more light. If 10,000 lumens are available at sight (the area where photosynthesis is occurring), stretching shouldn't be a problem. If your plants are stretching, give them more light. (Explanations about light can be found in Chapter 3, page 44.)

TIP: To determine the appropriate spacing from an air-cooled High Intensity Discharge (HID) system to the plants, use the back of your hand to determine the top of the growing area. Place your hand under the lamp and raise it until your skin feels uncomfortable. This is the top of the growing area; 6 to 8 inches below this is the bottom of the growing area. Making sure the tops of your plants are near the bottom of the growing area will ensure that they receive substantial amounts of light and have enough room to grow for 10 days or so in case you cannot return to your garden.

This young plant is in the second stage of vegetative growth.

When the third set of true leaves begins to form, the plant is transitioning into its second stage of vegetative growth. Commonly referred to as "starts," plants are in this stage from the time they grow the third set of true leaves until they reach ripeness to flower, at which time they're considered to be in the third stage of growth.

In the second stage, plants may receive a full dose of nutrient solution, as well as starches, carbohydrates, minerals, vitamins, and hormones. Remember that nitrogen is important during this stage and the N-P-K (nitrogen, phosphorous, potassium) ratio should be something like 4-3-3. Commercially sold nutrients labeled "Grow" will have this ratio, or have even more nitrogen depending on the formulation. The important part is that there needs to be more nitrogen than phosphorous in the nutrient solution. Nitrogen promotes healthy green growth, taking your starts into the third stage of vegetation with an ample store of all the vital nutrients necessary for the increasing demands of the explosive third stage of growth and the change to flowering.

Third Stage

The third stage of vegetative growth begins when a plant reaches its minimum maturity to begin flowering and fruiting, but the photoperiod keeps the plant from beginning to flower. Plants are larger than at their earlier stages, have well-established root systems, and have larger leaves to facilitate higher rates of photosynthesis. The ability of the larger, established plant to consume more nitrogen by feeding on stronger solutions more frequently, absorb larger amounts of CO_2, and use more light lead to the accelerated growth patterns usually associated with this stage of vegetative growth.

Your plants can be held in the third stage of vegetative growth as long as you want. Generally this is done by using the stasis technique (24 hours of constant light) or setting a photoperiod of 18 hours of light/6 hours of darkness—simulating summertime in a temperate climate zone.

Control your lights with an automatic timer and, if you are using an environmental technique that draws air from outside, make sure your environment is completely dark with no light leaking in. You can check this by standing in the room with the lights off. Then program your timer to turn lights off during the hottest part of the day, typically noon to 6:00 p.m. This will help you to mitigate high temperatures, easing energy consumption by the fans. Keep the room at 75°F and the humidity at the higher end of the optimum range, 55 to 60 percent. Most plants prefer a little bit more humidity during the third stage of vegetative growth. Large, heavily fed third stage plants with ample light have the greatest potential to benefit from CO_2 enhancement; 1300 PPM (parts per million) to 1500 PPM CO_2 is commonly used.

The plant to the far right is in the third stage of vegetative growth.

This flower is a week or two away from a final flush.

FLOWERING

Once your plant has reached the end of the second stage of vegetative growth, your plant will have developed enough to grow flowers, fruit, and seed as long as the proper environmental conditions, nutritional requirements, and pollination requirements are met.

To induce flowering in photoperiodic plants, set the automatic light timers so that there are 12 hours of darkness. This extended period of darkness is nature's way of telling your plants that it's "fall" (albeit artificial), and thus the end of their annual lifecycle is coming and reproduction is necessary.

The optimum temperature (OT) at this point in the plant's life cycle is still 75°F, but relative humidity (RH) in a room housing flowering cannabis plants should be kept at a strict 50 percent. Increased airflow, circulation, or a dehumidifier may be necessary to keep the humidity on the lower side. Lower humidity also helps keep molds and bacteria from taking up residence in the flowers. Light intensity is important at this point. The more light your plants receive at this stage, the larger and denser their flower formations will be.

Cannabis plants will continue to grow (lengthen) during the first half of flowering. This is commonly referred to as stretching, but don't confuse this with the lengthening of internodal space caused by low light levels (which is also called stretching). Remain attentive during flowering, moving lights accordingly until vertical growth has stopped completely.

Generally after vertical growth has stopped completely, the buds that formed in early flowering begin to swell and new buds form in denser growth patterns. This makes the plants top-heavy. You will have to support this weight by creating a trellising system, tying vertical supports to the stems, caging, or staking.

In plants where pollination occurs very early in flowering, seed production can begin before vertical growth has finished. This is common on herbaceous annuals, and if this has occurred, you will notice that some of the calyxes in the buds are not flowers, but pods containing husks with developing seeds in them. These plants have an early seed cycle to ensure another generation, but even these early-to-seed species produce flowers and pollinate normally, effectively doubling their chances of survival.

Buds swell as the flowering process continues, opening and revealing the reproductive parts designed for pollination (fertilization). Once pollinated, plants produce seeds.

HYBRIDS VS. NONHYBRIDS, SEXING THE PLANT

Sexing a plant is the practice of determining whether a dioecious plant is male or female. In cannabis plants, the female flower is preferred over the male flower for the end product. You do, however, need some male plants if you are planning to hybridize your own strains.

Once you determine the sex of the plants, it's important to separate the males and females. Knowing which plants are pollen producers and which ones are pollen receivers is usually the beginning of any breeding process. (And you don't want the plants to breed themselves if you're trying to achieve specific results.)

To properly determine the sex of a plant, nurture it until it reaches the third stage of vegetative growth, making sure it has undergone as little environmental stress as possible.

When the plant is mature enough to flower, change your nutrient solution from a nitrogen-heavy "grow" formula to a phosphorus-heavy "bloom" formula. Allow the plant to feed on this solution for 10 days before changing the photoperiod to 12 hours of light/12 hours of darkness a day. This is known as "chemical induction" or "chemically forcing" flowering, and it shifts the plant from vegetative growth to the blooming phase of its life in an efficient manner with minimal stress. Remember that stress slows down growth, so always avoid stressing plants if possible. In nature, the photoperiod changes slowly day by day, so longer induction periods (the time when you are making changes in conditions to induce changes in plant growth) may be necessary based on your desired results.

Once the plant is being fed a steady bloom solution and you've changed the photoperiod to one that will induce blooming, it is just a matter of time before the plant will flower. Then you can determine if the plants are males or females. It is important to *check the plants every day* for signs of flowering so that you can determine the sex of the plants and separate males from females before pollination happens.

Seven to 21 days after you change nutrient and photoperiod conditions to induce flowering, flowers will begin to form at the node regions of the main stem, between the axillary bud or the stipule.

MALE/FEMALE PARTS

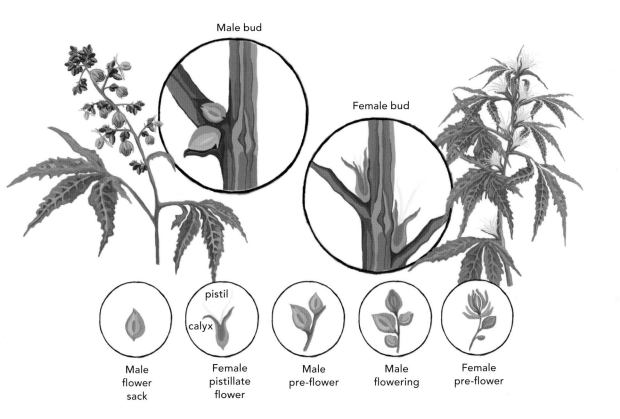

Male bud

Female bud

pistil

calyx

Male flower sack

Female pistillate flower

Male pre-flower

Male flowering

Female pre-flower

The males will form flowers with stamens containing the pollen; the female flowers form pistils, which consist of an ovary at the bottom, a style that projects forth and often looks like a hair or a very small shoot, and a sticky stigma at the top end to catch pollen.

Don't let pollen from male plants contaminate female plants, because once the females have been fertilized for seed production, it is difficult, if not impossible, to reverse the process. If you're planning to grow a plant to use as a mother (the plant from which you can take cuttings to root and grow for future crops), allowing it to be fertilized accidentally essentially ruins all of the hard work that you've put into it.

Occasionally a dioecious cannabis plant will produce both sexual organs on the same plant. Get rid of plants that do that. These self-pollinators, although often essential in nature to ensure survival of the species, are extremely problematic in a controlled production environment. They can pollinate entire rooms, driving all your plants to set seed instead of forming large buds for harvest or vegetative growth for propagation. Rogue plants will mix genetics in uncontrolled ways, making it impossible to keep track of breeding processes.

RE-VEGGING

Re-vegging for production purposes is the process of letting the plants flower, harvesting the flowers, then returning the remaining parts of the plant to vegetative growth. This cuts down on vegetation cycle length, as the plant already has a well-established root system. This can *greatly* increase the number of harvestable stalks the second or even third time around.

When plants return to the vegetative state, it is often the first time they undergo stress, and, depending on the structure of the plants' growth patterns, they may undergo a period of strange growth. Cannabis plants demonstrate polyfoliation, or multiple vegetative shoots growing from one bud. Leaves might curl or grow in strange shapes. Don't be alarmed—this is just the plant's natural reaction to unnatural changes it has gone through. As plants begin to grow again in a vegetative state, the hormone balances will be restored and the plants will grow normally.

First you harvest, but make sure to leave the bottom portion of branches intact so the plant can send out new growth. A good rule of thumb is to leave the bottom quarter of the plant untouched. The important part is to leave some nodes and/or buds, as they contain the meristems to create new growth. If you are using a horizontal trellis, you will most likely have several nodes and underdeveloped buds underneath the dense plane of flowers you have grown. You can harvest, then cut 4 to 6 inches of branches underneath the trellis away to allow room for the new growth.

The next step is to change your nutrient solution back to a nitrogen-dominant "grow" formula and your photoperiod to 24 (or 18/6) hours of light. This will signal to the plant that the conditions for vegetative growth are right. This pushes it to adjust its hormone levels accordingly and to produce new structural growth—stems and leaves instead of flowers. This process is stressful to plants and can cause strange changes as they return to vegetative growth. Don't be alarmed; this is just the plants' natural reaction to an unnatural situation.

Some things you might encounter are structural changes like parallel growth changing to alternate or vice versa; polyfoliation; changes in leaf structure like odd curling; margins that are smooth instead of serrated or vice versa; or mild or extreme vein, color, or textural changes in leaves. You could feed a tonic, a silicon additive, or a vitamin and mineral additive just after harvest to help combat stress and ease the changes happening inside the plants.

The final step is to grow your plants in a vegetative state until you are ready to induce flowering, and then harvest when the flowers reach the proper maturity. You can repeat this process as long as root zones remain healthy and you are getting desirable harvests.

RE-VEGGING

1: Harvest the plant, leaving the bottom quarter or so to grow new vegetation.

2: Feed a tonic, a silicon additive, a vitamin additive, or a combination of the three. You could also feed a nitrogen-dominant "grow" formula with these or by itself.

3: Return to a vegetative photoperiod (24 hours of light, or 18/6).

4: Grow in a vegetative state for the desired length of time.

5: When your plants are the desired size, change the photoperiod to 12/12 and feed a "bloom" formula, flowering just like normal.

6: Harvest when desired, and repeat as needed as long as root zones are healthy and you were happy with the last harvest.

MOTHERING AND CLONING

Mother plants are plants that are kept in stasis and grown for their lush vegetation in order to make many viable genetic copies of plants (clones) over long periods of time. This can be a uniquely demanding scenario, both for the gardener and for the plant. To keep the mother plant happy, you'll have to prune regularly to control aggressive growth and give the plant specific nutritional boosts to keep it healthy and/or help it recover from aggressive pruning. Cutting large numbers of clones periodically taxes the plant quite a bit.

Triggering Branching: FIM vs. Pinching

The first cutting technique you will need to be familiar with is a newer version of the heading technique known as the FIM technique. The FIM technique is the process of cutting the apical meristem (the terminal bud at the top of the plant, from which the plant grows vertically) in half using a 45-degree-angle cut instead of heading it (removing the whole apical meristem). This will give you the desired result with less stress to the plant.

Pinching, the other technique to trigger branching, is the process of removing the terminal bud at the end of a shoot to displace the hormones in that shoot, allowing the lower buds to grow into terminal buds forming shoots themselves.

Clinical trials of the FIM technique vs. pinching have shown that they result in the same structural changes, but the FIM produces higher yields overall. Both techniques work well for turning a vertical-growing plant into a bushy mother. If yield (more clones), health of the plant, and shock are major concerns, use the FIM technique.

The plant should recover quickly from this type of stress, but it will no longer grow vertically from its main stem. When the cut heals over, that's it. The buds positioned lower on the plant will break and begin to grow, creating a bushier plant. This is what you want—multiple shoots that are viable for cuttings.

If you wish to root another genetic copy to turn into a second mother, simply cut a clone.

Pinching is simply removing the terminal bud on a shoot by delicately pinching it off by hand.

HOW TO: ASEXUAL REPRODUCTION (CLONING)

Asexual reproduction is the propagation of plants by taking cuttings from a section of the plant and inducing roots to grow from the bottom of that cutting. This type of reproduction is asexual because pollen and the sexual organs of the plants are not involved.

The mother is the plant from which the cuttings are taken. The clones (cuttings) are called daughters. The daughter plants are considered to be the same age as the mother. For instance, if the mother is one year old, mature to ripe, and a cutting is taken, that daughter is also one year old and, even though it is small in size, as soon as it has roots it is possible to bring it directly into bloom, creating one short, compact flower or clusters of flowers depending on the structure.

To root clones you will need the following equipment:

- 10x20-inch propagation tray
- 7-inch propagation dome
- Propagation medium (compressed bark plugs or mat, low-density high-drainage foam, rock wool, or coir pellets)
- Scalpels
- Rooting gel that contains IBA (indole-3butyrcic acid) and NAA (naphthalene acetic acid)
- Clean spray bottle

Before you start, it is important to make sure your equipment is sterile, especially your scalpel. Cuttings are prone to disease and fungal infections. They often end up with rust, smut, or damping off (all plant diseases), and can develop necrosis or even botrytis. More often than not, a dirty scalpel is the culprit.

STERILIZE THE SCALPEL

To clean a scalpel, bring it to 500°F for ten seconds by holding it in a flame (from a cigarette lighter, for example) for 20 seconds or so. Then wipe it on a clean piece of cloth or tissue. You can also let it sit in isopropyl alcohol for about the same amount of time. Professional growers sometimes forgo this and never use the same tool twice, but that is not a very cost-effective technique.

Next decide if you want each individual cutting to go directly into the medium of choice or be placed into a bowl of tepid water to continue the process one step at a time. Using a bowl of water can be easier, but doing so puts the cuttings at greater risk of developing an embolism. An embolism is an air pocket that forms in the freshly cut stem either in the cambium layer, the xylem, or phloem. This almost always destroys any chance that the clone will survive and makes it a carrier for disease and fungus as it fails to root. Clones either root or rot, and unfortunately the rotting can be contagious, so avoid embolisms by using a *sharp* scalpel or razor to make a clean slice. Do not use scissors, which can crush the stems, allowing cracks and air pockets to develop. Always make your cuts at a 45-degree angle; this will keep the stem from closing off the roots you want to form from the xylem and phloem, and give you a better surface area for hormone application.

You must move through the cutting process in a quick, concise manner, so familiarize yourself with these steps before attempting asexual production.

Cloning Step by Step

Use a mother with branch structure with at least ten nodes or branches. This will allow you ample room to take a cutting, and the remaining stock will have enough branches to begin the mothering process.

1. Lay out your tray, medium of choice, cutting tool, container of gel, and a waste receptacle for the foliage you will be cutting away when you clean up the clones. Put this within arm's reach of the mother plant you intend on using. It is easiest to work on one direction (left to right, or vice versa) so place your equipment in this order: mother, waste receptacle, gel container, medium, and tray. This will allow you to work quickly and efficiently to avoid embolisms.

2. Pour an ounce or two of gel from its original container into a clean container to work in. Never use the original gel container as this has a chance to inoculate the gel with fungus or disease, ruining it for future use. Use the working container to keep your gel clean and sterile to use later.

3. Pour ½ inch of tepid water into the bottom of the tray. (You can pour it in along the edge.) It is important to promote moisture in the cloning environment for elevated humidity levels. Your medium will use capillary action to pull this water up and help root development. Never hand-water your cloning medium, as this will wash away the rooting gel, making it harder for roots to form.

4. Starting from the meristem, or tip of the branch, count down four branches and internode spaces. At the top of the fifth node, just above any auxiliary buds, make your incision.

5. Make a 45-degree-angle cut just above this node. Do not leave excess stem in place above the sixth node, as this will rot and invite bugs, fungi, and disease. The 45-degree-angle cut ensures that enough surface area of the cambium, xylem, and phloem are exposed in order to apply hormone to it, and doesn't send the signals to the plant to close the wound as quickly with scar tissue.

6. Holding the cutting gently in your off hand, being careful not to crush the stem, use your cutting tool to remove the lower two branches where they connect to the main stem. Again, do not leave excess stem material; make nice clean cuts as close to the stem as possible without cutting into it. This removes these lower branches so you have something to place into the medium, and it promotes vertical growth.

7. Grab your working gel container. Still holding the cutting firmly, but not crushing the stem, set down your scalpel on a clean surface and dip the 45-degree-angled cut directly into the gel. Using a scooping motion, make sure a liberal amount of gel covers the entire cut and to about ¼ inch above the cut.

CLONING STEPS

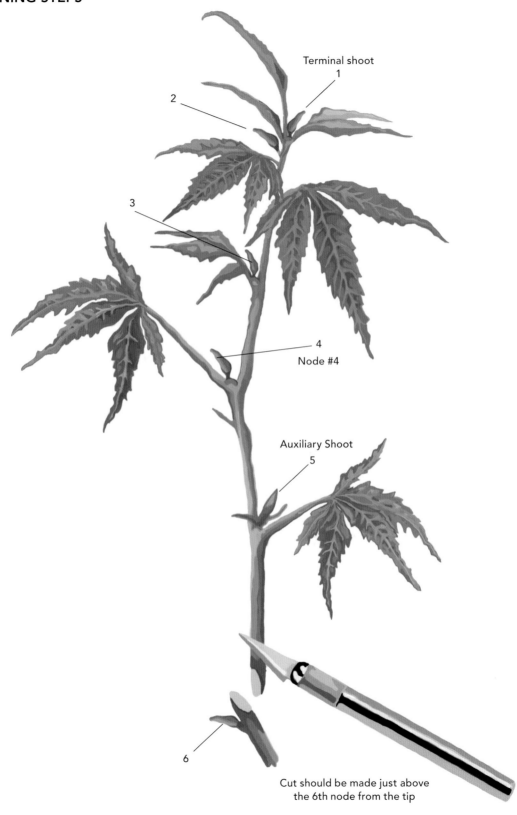

Terminal shoot
1

2

3

4
Node #4

Auxiliary Shoot
5

6

Cut should be made just above
the 6th node from the tip

8. Place your cutting, cut end first, into the medium to a depth of ⅔ to ⅘ the depth of the medium. Too deep and the gel will wash away, too shallow and the cutting could tip over or dry out easily. This depth ensures stability as well as enough spacing for roots to grow out and down.

9. Repeat Steps 4–7 with other branches on plants that have viable sites to remove cuttings.

10. When all desired cuttings have been taken, cleaned (lower branches removed), dipped in gel, and placed in a medium, spray the foliage, the medium, and the inside of the dome liberally with plain tepid water.

11. Place the dome on top of the tray so that it fits snug and ensures all vents are closed. This will give you the desired humidity.

While the roots are forming, the new clones will be feeding from the moisture in the air. This is known as foliar feeding and is their only option with no roots. It is important to keep them within the proper range for temperature and humidity, 75°F to 90°F for temperature and as close to 99 percent humidity as possible. Wetting the medium from the top by spraying it and from the bottom from standing water ensures the proper moisture for roots to form and doesn't wash away the hormones in the gel.

It takes anywhere from 10 to 21 days for roots to form. During this time clones are very fragile and should never be allowed to dry out. Water or check every day to ensure they have the proper humidity. Remove the dome, check the standing water level and the medium moisture, and spray the foliage and the inside of the dome before closing everything back up.

Do not feed clones with a nutrient solution even if they appear yellow or spotty; it is easy to burn them and the roots are vulnerable. As soon as the roots push out of the medium and down into the tray, the clones can be removed and fed a half-strength solution for one cycle in any irrigation system. The second cycle can be full strength, but it may be to your advantage to allow a young "net" of 3- to 4-inch roots to form over a week or two, depending on species.

Allow 20 days or so from the time you cut the apical meristem for the plant to heal, recover, and further develop nodes and shoots. Around this time you should be able to remove a cutting from each shoot. Count the nodes on the shoots starting from the terminal bud. You will be removing the first five, so any that remain below that will form into the new shoots in 20 more days. Let's say nine nodes have formed during this 20-day period, so after removing clones you are left with four nodes on each branch. Eight shoots multiplied by four nodes each plus 20 days will give you thirty-two new shoots to clone ($S \times N = C$). Repeating this process again will yield 128 clones in 20 more days.

To start with, a full-strength grow solution, rich in nitrogen, and a vitamin and hormone supplement will be enough to provide proper nutrition and protection from stress. A liquid synthetic vitamin solution will work well, administered at least every other cycle to keep nutrient sinks (where plants store nutrients inside of cells) full and healthy. An organic alternative is an extract of Norwegian kelp, which contains some similar chemical compounds. Specific mother plant nutrient solutions are also available and usually have an N-P-K ratio of 1.5-.5-1.5 to promote healthy growth and fight stress, but they do not contain the essential vitamins and hormones to protect from the wide range of things that can go wrong, so you are better off using your normal grow solution plus the vitamin/hormone additive. If stress gets to be too much and growth becomes weak, if fungi or disease take hold, or if you just wish to reinvigorate your mother periodically, you can feed it a plant tonic such as Advanced Nutrients Revive or Thrive Alive by Technaflora, or mix your own by combining carbohydrates, potassium, a silicate, vitamins, and minerals (synthetic or kelp extract), trace amounts of calcium, magnesium, and iron as well as your normal grow solution.

Whatever you choose to correct problems or reinvigorate, remember to be attentive and not overdue it.

Watch for recovery and then return to your regular feeding schedule. The point is to refill sinks, promote quick recovery, and encourage new, fresh green growth. Using these nutritional techniques combined with an indefinite vegetative environment (stasis), you can produce more and healthier clones cycle after cycle, from the same mother, for long periods, even for years!

Maintaining a mother plant in terms of environmental conditions, nutritional needs, and space concerns is an art form. The important thing to remember is that the nodes you leave when you take a clone will form the shoots that you will later take clones from.

Pruning the Mother

When a mother begins to outgrow its space, it is a good opportunity to practice your pruning techniques. Thinning is usually the first line of defense against the mother outgrowing your reproduction chamber. Simply cut branches or shoots that are failing to compete properly for light in order to open up room for new growth. Cut them close to the main stem to avoid leaving a nub (those will attract disease, fungus, and pests). Topping can be used to give a shortening and widening effect; simply go down a couple of branches from the top and make a 45-degree-angle cut on the main stem. This is rough on the mother, so pay attention afterward, at least until the cut scabs over.

GROWING A NEW MOTHER

If the pressure of mothering becomes too great for your plant, and growth becomes weak yielding thin, sickly shoots that aren't ideal for cloning, don't be afraid to make a new mother. For production purposes, you may want to plan ahead for this as the sharp reduction in the number of clones being produced will directly affect yield, which can be a problem if you're on a strict schedule.

Take the strongest clone from the previous set of cuttings and replace the worn-out mother with it; it's that simple. There is a wives' tale that has been floating around the industry for the last twenty-five years or so that the genetic quality of plants suffers over time in this process, and after five or six replacement mothers, your plants become weakened to disease and pests and even produce less. This simply isn't true. Remember that the plant has a kind of biological memory in terms of its overall age, so over time, multiple stress periods from poor care can have this effect.

Be kind to your plants, keeping them strong and as stress free as possible, and they will produce for you indefinitely.

The next chapter covers the environmental factors that affect plant growth. Now that you understand the stages of growth, you can learn how to manipulate environmental conditions to affect the plant growth.

Choose a vigorous, healthy plant to serve as the mother and take care not to over- or underprune it.

CHAPTER 3

Environmental Factors Affecting Plant Growth

Environmental conditions that affect indoor gardens are similar to those affecting outdoor gardens, but indoors, unlike with outdoor gardens, you, the grower, have control over these factors and can manipulate them to influence plant growth instead of reacting to them as you would outdoors.

When setting up and using your hydroponic system, these are the environmental factors that you'll need to monitor and adjust:

- Water
- Nutrient availability
- Light
- Temperature
- Humidity
- CO_2 and circulation

The key to successfully growing marijuana indoors hydroponically is, as much as possible, to keep these factors as close to the conditions that marijuana plants grow best at. The important thing to remember is that the environmental conditions are so interrelated that changes in one condition will result in changes in another.

Opposite: Temperature, light, humidity, and ventilation are the primary factors you'll need to control in your growing environment.

Let's say, for example, humidity gets too low and the stomata close. Respiration (CO_2 uptake) will grind to a halt, and photosynthesis (the processing of light) will decrease and become less efficient, thus affecting nutrient uptake, all of which will result in stunted growth and visibly wilted plants. Optimum temperature within the plant will quickly become too high, increasing the severity of the situation. In a flowering state, plants can exist like this for some time, but in a 24-hour vegetative state, death can occur quickly.

There are any number of scenarios like this that can happen. Power can fail, making the lights turn off or watering systems shut down, among other things. Know your environment and make it a point to stay two steps ahead of these scenarios, but remember, it happens to everyone eventually, whether from power failures, miscalculations, or just plain old negligence. Just treat these setbacks as valuable learning experiences instead of beating yourself up or throwing in the towel.

WATER

Water is the backbone of every hydroponic garden. And whether you know it or not, all water is *not* created equally, and some is better than others for hydroponic systems. The four water conditions that are paramount to a successful garden are:

- Potential hydrogen (pH)
- Electrical conductivity (EC) or parts per million (PPM) of dissolved salts and measurable contaminants
- Temperature
- Oxygen levels

WHAT IS pH?

In nutrient solutions, pH (potential Hydrogen) works exactly the same way as it does in soil. It is defined as the negative logarithm of the hydrogen ion concentration in the medium being measured. The pH scale ranges from 0–14. Readings below 7 are acidic; 7 is neutral; and readings above 7 are alkaline. The typical pH range for a hydroponic nutrient solution is between 5.8 to 6.2, or 6.0 to 6.8 for soil or coco coir. Always avoid extremes; nutrient lockout occurs with pH levels that are both too high and too low. Many instances of overdoses and deficiencies are a result of pH being out of range. It is a shame to have nutrients in ample supply but not reaching the plants due to extremes in pH.

The pH of the solution can be regulated with synthetic or organic methods. Use potassium hydroxide to raise pH and nitric acid to lower pH. It is important to remember that when you add these things to your solution it affects the EC/PPM, so try to keep track of the rate at which measured amounts

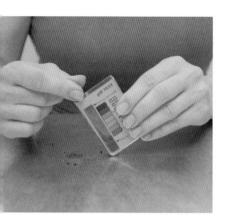

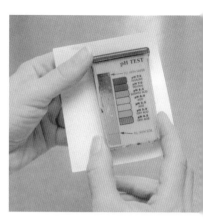

of the solution you add will change the pH. This will help you avoid adding too much of one, therefore needing to amend with the other, and thereby unnecessarily increasing the EC/PPM of the solution.

It's easy to test coir pH with a simple pH kit.

PPM, EC, AND TDS

PPM (parts per million), EC (electrical conductivity), and TDS (total dissolved solids) are three different ways to measure solids in a nutrient solution. These measurements do not tell you what is in your solution/water; they are merely indicators of its ability to conduct electricity. Even supposedly "clean" tap water contains chlorine/chloramines, sediment, rust, volatile organic compounds (VOCs), bacteria, iron, sulfur, and fluoride. Many urban water sources dispense "hard water" containing high levels of calcium and magnesium, making EC/PPM high. Any and all of these contaminants can cause problems with growth by killing beneficial fungi and bacteria, locking out key nutrients, adversely affecting nutrient uptake, or encouraging pathogens strong enough to survive chlorine and fluoride to take hold and prosper.

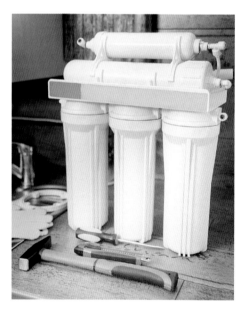

Expensive water tests or water testing equipment can be purchased to determine the levels and types of contaminants, but the less expensive and more realistic solution is to clean your water using reverse osmosis. The best thing to do is use a reverse osmosis unit (available at home-improvement centers or through a local or online hydroponics shop) to clean your water and lower the EC/PPM, then build the nutrient solution from scratch around the needs of the plant. Avoid the cheaper de-chlorination and sediment filter equipment, as those only remove chlorine, sediment, and rust. Reverse osmosis machines remove all contaminants and 98

Water purification equipment is ready to install.

percent of bacteria, reduce PPM by 95 percent, and cost only a few dollars more. In addition, ultraviolet light can be used to kill 100percent of bacteria. These are available at feed stores and through online hydroponics stores.

OXYGEN

Oxygen is one of the elements that you can't really have too much of, at least in your water. Oxygen in the water/nutrient solution extends the life of your nutrients, protects against anaerobic bacteria, and optimizes the effectiveness of your plants' root systems.

Expensive oxygen generators can be used, but I recommend aquarium-style air pumps with ceramic air stones. It is easy to judge whether the water has proper oxygen levels by looking at the water. Ideally the water should have the kind of bubbles and ratio of bubbles to water seen in a clear carbonated beverage. I call this the "Sprite" look. If you have it, you are good; if not, increase the oxygenation by adding another pump and stone. An important safety tip is to keep the pump, or at least the line running air to the stone, well above the solution to keep the water from getting into the pump and causing an electrical fire.

NUTRIENT AVAILABILITY

Nutrients feed plants and facilitate photosynthesis, cell division, and respiration. There is a huge market for hydroponic nutrients, with dozens of companies all claiming their solutions are the answer to higher yields. It is important to realize that there is no ideal mixture of salts for hydroponic solutions. For any plant species, there is a wide range of ideal nutrient availability. Favorable levels for a particular species vary according to environmental conditions, especially temperature and light intensity. Keep this in mind when reading sales pitches for different solutions. The composition of the nutrient product is more important than any sales claims.

Nutrients are classified as either macronutrients or micronutrients.

Macronutrients
- Nitrogen (N)
- Phosphorus (P)
- Potassium (K)
- Calcium (Ca)
- Sulfur (S)

Micronutrients

- Magnesium (M)
- Iron (Fe)
- Manganese (Mn)
- Boron (B)
- Zinc (Zn)
- Copper (Cu)
- Molybdenum (Mo)
- Chlorine (Cl)

These nutrients are available as organic or synthetic formulas and, more recently, as combinations of both synthetics and organics referred to as "hybrid solutions." Synthetic nutrients are usually salt based. Products claiming to be organic are usually hybrids that contain organic ingredients with one or more dissolved salts to bolster performance. Truly organic nutrients will have a label saying they are OMRI listed. OMRI is an acronym for Organic Materials Review Institute. If you want to claim that you're growing organically, every product you use should be listed with this organization.

Manufacturers offer solid and liquid forms of nutrients. Sometimes the nutrients are sold in packages with two or three different containers or packages that you mix together. Three-part nutrients give you greater control over the end N-P-K ratio of the solution. Two-part nutrients contain substances that are charged differently and, if mixed together in concentrated form, will react chemically and form hard salts. One-part solutions use a chemical to keep this reaction from happening or use ingredients that don't react to each other, offering a simple "dilute and use" alternative for novices.

Nutritional supplements and additives can bolster microbial activity at the root zone; increase size, flavor, and aroma; aid in recovery from stress or damage; and increase essential oil production, among other things. Optimum environmental conditions, the appropriate amount of macronutrients and micronutrients, and careful selection of additives and supplements are the essential equation to reaching a plant's genetic potential and achieving maximum results.

If nutrients are deficient in a solution or overabundant (hot), you will undoubtedly see curling, yellowing, or burning of leaves. You don't want to over- or underfertilize, so always follow the manufacturer's recommendations with any new nutrient additives or supplements. Keep in mind that the ratio of N-P-K that a plant needs changes throughout the course of a plant's life. Plants use more nitrogen during vegetative growth and more phosphorous during flowering.

The most effective way to monitor what your plants need and are able to use is to keep track of the PPM of the solution. At the beginning of the feeding cycle note the PPM, then measure it again at a chosen interval (24 hours, again at 5 days, then before changing the solution), keeping track of how much the number drops. If the pH hasn't fallen or increased significantly, affecting uptake, this is an accurate way to see how much your plants are "eating." You can use a meter to measure PPM. These are available at hydroponics stores.

LIGHT

All plants require light to grow and bloom. Most photosensitive plants initiate their flowering stage of growth when they receive 12 hours of light and 12 hours of darkness. Vegetative growth can be facilitated 24 hours a day or at 18 hours of light and 6 hours of darkness. I've found that darkness is unnecessary for vegetative growth, seeding, and cuttings, but old habits die hard and many indoor growers still insist on a dark period.

TIP: Plants do not use the spectrum of light that appears green to us, so you can use a green linear or CFL as a work light in a flowering garden. (These lights are available online. These aren't grow lights; in fact, they are the opposite of grow lights.) Do not "wake up" sleeping plants; this is known as light stress and can slow flowering, lead to hormone imbalances, and even limit yields. Observing this practice is known as light discipline.

Plants grow and bloom according to the amount of light they receive. Light intensity is measured in lumens or foot-candles (1 foot-candle = lumen/ft^2). Lumens are a measure of light output. The lumens measurement of a light source does not change depending on where the light is placed. It is a fixed number per bulb. Foot-candles indicates the amount of light emitted by one candle that falls on 1 square foot of surface located at the distance of 1 foot from the candle. Traditionally lumens have been the benchmark of a lamp's ability to grow plants, meaning the brighter the lamp, the better the plant. However, studies have shown that a broader color spectrum lamp will perform much better than a lamp with high lumen output and a narrow color spectrum, especially when it comes to plant growth. Optimum range for growth begins at 10,000 lumens at site, but the general rule of thumb with light is: the more lumens in the appropriate spectrum, the better.

Only part of solar radiation is used by plants for photosynthesis. The photosynthetically active radiation (PAR) includes the wavelengths between 400 to 700 nanometers and falls just within the so-called visible spectrum (which is 380–770 nanometer). The total visible spectrum is perceived by humans as "white" light, but with the aid of a prism, we see that the "white" light is actually separated into a spectrum of colors from violet to blue to green, yellow, orange, and red.

Plants use the blue to red light as their energy source for photosynthesis. Color temperature (K) is a way to measure the spectrum of an indoor lamp. It is the relative whiteness of a piece of tungsten steel heated to that temperature in degrees Kelvin, not how hot the lamp is. Heating the steel to 2700°K makes the color red/orange, at 4200°K the steel turns blue, and around 6500°K it gets bright blue/white.

LIGHT PAR

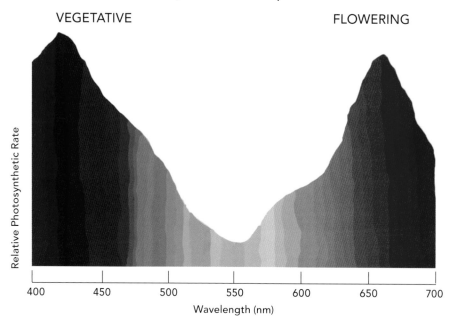

Photosynthetic Action Spectrum

VEGETATIVE   FLOWERING

Relative Photosynthetic Rate

400   450   500   550   600   650   700

Wavelength (nm)

When choosing indoor lighting, spectrum should be your first consideration. Next, heat vs. lumen output will determine the wattage of lamp you'll want for your particular environment. Don't overshoot your environment's cooling capacity, as this causes temperature and humidity problems that are difficult to correct, turning the environment into a "hot house" that grows bugs and unwanted fungi better than plants.

When the light is on, the brighter the better is the rule. It is easy, however, to have too much heat emanating from the lamp. A good way to tell if the lamp is going to emit so much heat that it will burn the plants is to place your hand, palm down, over the top of the plant. If the top of your hand is hot, you need to raise the lamp. As the plants grow larger you will need to raise the lamp again.

Air-cooled reflectors allow you to keep a lamp much cooler by enclosing it in tempered glass and using fans to evacuate the excess heat. I've actually cooled a 400-watt HPS lamp, using fans, to the point where I could hold my hand to the tempered glass plate indefinitely, without fear of burning myself, and thus let the plants grow right up to the glass.

As light moves away from its source, it diminishes as follows: 1/Distance × Distance. This is known as "the inverse property of light." For example 1 foot = 1000FC (foot-candles), 2 feet = 250FC, 3 feet = 111FC, 4 feet = 63FC, 5 feet = 40FC, 6 feet = 28FC, and so forth. Your goal is to maximize the lumens by getting your lamps as cool as possible so you can position the lamps as close to the plants as possible. Remember: the closer you get to your plants, the smaller the

A 2x2-foot flowering closet.

An open veg area with a T5 lamp.

area the lamp can cover. That is the tradeoff everyone has to deal with: area for lumens or vice versa. Typical mounting heights are 12 to 24 inches above the plants for low-wattage systems, 12 to 36 inches above the plants for medium-watt systems, and 18 to 48 inches above the plants for high-wattage systems.

Using these heights, the average coverage area by wattage for HID lamps is 8×8 feet for 1000 watts, 6.5×6.5 feet for 600 watts, 4×4 feet for 400 watts, 3×3 feet for 320 watts, and a 2×2 feet area for 175/150 watts.

HID stands for high intensity discharge, which is a special type of lighting that is much more intense (brighter) than other types of lighting available. An HID lighting system consists of a ballast, reflector, socket, and lamp (light bulb). The ballast acts like an engine, converting and driving energy to illuminate the lamp. HID lamp options include high-pressure sodium (HPS), metal halide (MH), mercury vapor, and low-pressure sodium.

The two typically used for plant growth are HPS and MH systems. MH lamps provide more of the blue/green spectrum, which is ideal for leafy crops and/or plants that are in a vegetative stage (actively growing in size). MH lamps provide a color range similar to sunlight and are typically the choice for plants that have little or no natural light available.

HPS lamps provide more yellow/orange/red spectrum, which is ideal for most plants that are actively fruiting and/or flowering. In addition, HPS lighting is the choice for growers looking to supplement natural sunlight. In an ideal situation, you'd use both types of lamps. This is called "dual spectrum." There are some special bulbs that can do this in one socket if heat or electricity are major concerns.

Fluorescents range in size from T12 to T5VHO (very high output). T12s are typically used for overhead lighting and are the oldest and least efficient at about 30 lumens per watt. T8s are slightly smaller and more efficient. With the advent of T8HO bulbs that fit into any standard 4-foot T8 fixture and put out 88 lumens per watt, they are the most economical choice for the gardener on a budget and work great for starting seeds and cuttings.

T5HO are excellent for starting seeds, cuttings, and even young plants with a 92.6 lumen-to-watt ratio and the minimum heat output of a fluorescent. The newest are the T5VHO lamps that offer 95 lumens per watt, making them viable for full-term growth, but they emit just enough heat to require them to be air cooled, and they cost as much as most HID lamps. Compact fluorescent lights (CFL) are self-ballasted, but even though they are four times stronger than incandescent, or household light bulbs, at 42 watts, the initial lumens are only 2700, which is not enough for the kind of growth you want in your plants. The larger CFLs, known as high-wattage self-ballasted grow lamps, range from 125 to 250 watts and are excellent for starting seeds and use over small garden areas, but at only 70 lumens per watt they aren't very efficient.

Incandescent light bulbs are not a viable option for growing plants. They have low output in the wrong spectrum.

TEMPERATURE

The optimum temperature for marijuana plant growth is 68°F to 75°F. You will notice this range is only 8°F.

Air cooling an indoor room is the preferred way to achieve temperature consistency with HID lamps. Careful consideration should be taken during the dark period of flowering plants as the main source of heat is usually a lamp and you don't want to shock or kill your plants when the lamps aren't on. Exhaust fans can be slowed via a thermostat or put on a timer and run for intervals to keep in enough heat.

Temperature is important because beneficial bacteria, fungi, and the proper availability of nutrients depend on water being in the tepid range. The temperature of tepid water is between 60°F to 80°F. Staying in this range facilitates the appropriate chemical processes for nutrient use and eases shock to the roots caused by a solution that is too hot or too cold. Organic nutrient solutions depend on beneficial microbiology for nutrient uptake. Low temperatures slow this microbiology down and high temperatures can literally cook beneficial microbes to death. An inexpensive aquarium heater and thermometer are the best equipment you can use to regulate the temperature of the nutrient solution.

CO2 CIRCULATION

BLOOM (4x8 tent)

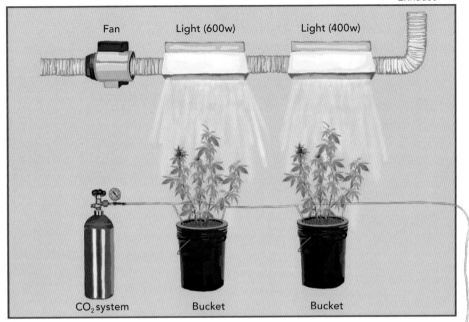

Exhaust

Fan   Light (600w)   Light (400w)

CO_2 system   Bucket   Bucket

VEG (4x4 tent)

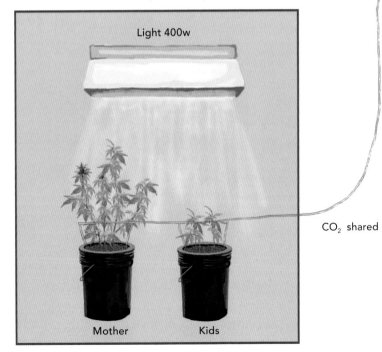

Light 400w

CO_2 shared

Mother   Kids

HUMIDITY

Relative humidity (RH) is the ratio between the amount of moisture in the air and the greatest amount of moisture the air *could* hold at a particular temperature. So an RH 50 percent reading at 75°F means that the air is currently holding half of the moisture that it could hold at a temperature of 75°F. As the temperature rises, air can hold more moisture than when it is a lower temperature. Moisture suspended in hot air being cooled will condense (the moisture particles will stick together). Outside, that condensation causes rain—or moisture falling out of the air.

The optimum range for RH falls between 40 to 60 percent. Higher humidity can lead to problems with fungi and diseases. Humidity at 70 percent and above is the optimum range for growth of most molds and diseases. Humidity can be controlled with dehumidifiers and humidifiers, portable commercial air conditioners, stationary home air conditioners, or, more simply, through proper circulation and strict monitoring of all other environmental conditions. Humidity discipline is the practice of controlling RH through passive means. It includes using a lid on reservoirs and planters to protect your solution from evaporation—which raises your RH and concentrates your solution—as well as cleaning up leaks and minimizing the use of foliar sprays.

CO_2 AND CIRCULATION

Plants need carbon dioxide (CO_2) to grow. A growing space with the appropriate amount of air circulation/exchange will provide plants with 300 to 400 PPM of CO_2, similar to what is available in nature. In greenhouses or indoors, fans are used to move in fresh air and move out stale air. If fans are run constantly, this process is referred to as "circulation." It is important to note that proper circulation pushes more air into a space than is evacuated/exhausted, leaving it positively charged. This gives the plants ample CO_2 and an opportunity to consume it via respiration, before the air is pulled out.

With temperature and humidity in optimum range plants can use 1300–1500 PPM of CO_2 to accelerate growth up to 150 percent. This is accomplished by flooding a given space with CO_2 using a CO_2 generator or a quick-release system. CO_2 generators use liquid propane or natural gas to run a number of burners creating CO_2. This is the most economic and effective way to enhance CO_2, but the vast majority of generators will increase the temperature of a 300-cubic-foot space by approximately 8°F. Quick-release systems use regulators to release CO_2 from compressed air tanks, not creating any heat, but costing considerably more in the long run.

Constant circulation paired with CO_2 enhancement would be a huge waste, because you'd be venting out all the CO_2-rich air before plants had a chance to use it. Use an interval circulation system if you're providing CO_2 enhancement. Connect fans to timers and run the fans in timed intervals, typically 15 minutes.

Left: Multiple venting strategies are required in most growing environments; you'll need inline fans in your ductwork as well as standalone fans (oscillating fans are a good choice) to create air movement within the growing area.

Opposite: Don't run fans constantly or the CO_2 will be vented before plants can use it. Connect fans to timers.

A cycle would look like this: 15 minutes CO_2 in, 30 minutes ambient (no circulation), 15 minutes out—or 15 minutes in, 15 minutes out to give plants time to utilize the CO_2 . Closed-loop systems and recent developments in water cooling of lights and CO_2 generators have made enclosed rooms a possibility. With no exhaust, CO_2 can be kept at high levels more cost-effectively (meaning you aren't losing CO_2 that hasn't been taken up by the plants through ventilation).

Temperature, RH, and CO_2 can be pushed to a state of enhancement above the usual optimum range, manipulating plant respiration into a state of hyperactivity and increasing growth even more. These parameters are 2000+ PPM CO_2, RH 65 to 75 percent, and temperatures 85°F to 95°F. Extreme care should be taken when using this technique; it can be tricky to maintain. It can also become a fertile breeding ground for molds, but as long as the CO_2 stays at 2000+ PPM, bugs have extreme difficulty surviving.

Now that you have a better understanding of the environmental factors affecting plant growth, you can learn about growing medium—the substance in which the plants will actually grow.

CHAPTER 4

Growing Media

When people think "hydroponics," they primarily think of plants growing in water without any soil. This encompasses the water culture techniques. Hydroponic systems fall into two categories: systems that use soilless growing media (a substance in which the plants grow) and systems in which the plants are suspended in a container via a neoprene or cork insert and the roots are sprayed or immersed in the nutrient solution (water culture). Hydroponic growing media help keep the plants in place, hold moisture and air, and can even be ecosystems for beneficial microbial life. Growing media is an integral part of many hydroponic systems. One can think of the water culture techniques as simply using air or oxygenated water (no growing medium, essentially) as a medium.

This flood table uses expanded clay pellets. A rock wool cube sits in the foreground.

Opposite: Some hydroponic systems suspend plants and their root structures directly in nutrient-enhanced water, but many rely on a soilless growing medium to help the plant achieve its growth potential.

There are many different types of media used for soilless cultures. Sand, gravel, siliceous rock (perlite), expanded clay pellets (hydroton), rock wool, coco coir, pressed composted tree bark (plugs), and, more recently, low-density, high-drainage foams. Each medium has different properties for water-to-air ratio, water retention, initial pH, pH stability nutrient retention, and capillary effect. These characteristics, combined with a plant's capacity for nutrient and water uptake, are used to determine the preferred frequency and type of irrigation to be used.

CHARACTERISTICS OF GROWING MEDIA
Water-to-Air Ratio
The water-to-air ratio, or resting saturation rate, is a measurement of how much air is trapped by porous chambers in a particular medium when it is fully saturated with water. (Media is fully saturated when it is completely submerged in water.) Oxygen in the root zone is vital to plant functioning. The more air that is stored in the growing media, the more often you can run the watering system to feed the plants (because you won't have to wait as long for the media to dry out).

Water Retention
Water retention is a measurement of how quickly a medium dries out after saturation. Wet and dry cycles dictate the structure of your plants' root systems. Wetter root zones produce longer roots with fewer root hairs. Drier root zones produce shorter roots with more root hairs. The healthiest root systems have a balance of length and root hairs, thereby creating maximum surface area to take advantage of oxygen and nutrients. You can ensure healthy root

WATER TO AIR

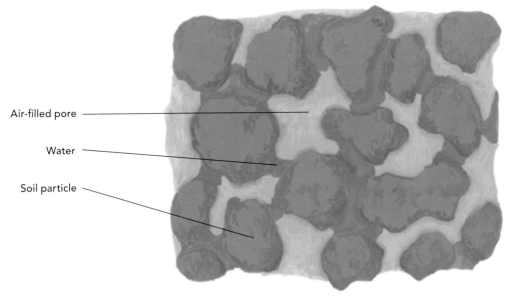

Air-filled pore

Water

Soil particle

growth by using the appropriate irrigation technique and feeding cycle for your specific growing media and plant.

Nutrient Retention

Nutrient retention is the measurement of a growing media's ability to hold cations and anions in between feeding cycles, thus making the nutrients available during dry periods.

pH Sustainability

pH sustainability is a growing media's ability to stay at the desired pH level as the feeding cycle progresses and nutrient retention within the media takes place. It is often referred to as pH buffering. Initial pH is the media's pH right out of the package, or before use. Although most media are inert (holding no initial nutrients) and neutral (pH 7), it is always a good idea to check the medium yourself with the proper measuring equipment to be sure. To test, get a container with 2cups of water in it. Test the pH and EC/TDS/PPM of the water. Add the medium to the water, agitate it momentarily, then test again. Results should be the same as the water without the medium. If it is not, rinse the medium until it passes the test.

Capillary Effect

Capillary effect is the ability of the media to move water in a passive manner. It is the movement of water within the spaces of a porous material due to the forces of adhesion, cohesion, and surface tension. *Cohesion* is water molecules sticking together. *Adhesion* is the term used for water molecules sticking to the media. Capillary action occurs when the attraction of the water molecules to the media is greater than the water molecules to one another.

CAPILLARY ACTION

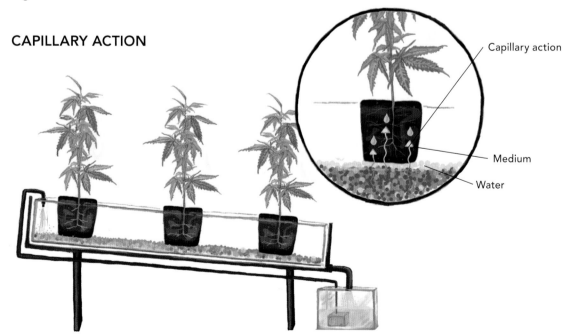

Capillary action

Medium

Water

TYPES OF GROWING MEDIA
Sand and Gravel

Sand is the original soilless culture medium, used since 1851 to grow plants in a nutrient solution. Coarse sand or gravel, cinders, crushed rock, and pumice all fall into this category. Individual particles can vary in size from ⅙ to ⅜ inches (4.2 to 9.5 millimeters). The water-to-air ratio of sand is low to nonexistent at the state of resting saturation. It is important, when growing in sand, to ensure that the nutrient solution is properly aerated.

The smaller the particles in this media, the better the water retention, capillary effect, and nutrient retention will be. This increases pH sustainability to some degree, but will always be relatively low compared to other soilless media. Media with larger particles have almost no pH sustainability. Sand and gravel are denser than other soilless media, making them heavier by volume.

COMPATIBLE SYSTEMS
Sand: Hand-watering, drip irrigation, wick irrigation
Gravel: Subirrigation

Siliceous Volcanic Rock (Perlite)

Perlite is a naturally occurring siliceous volcanic rock that when heated to 1600°F expands to twenty times its original volume. The kilning process is similar to popping popcorn and produces a growing medium that is sterile and has a neutral pH. It is similar to large gravel particles except it is lighter and has porosity, making its capillary effect, water-to-air ratio, and nutrient retention better than sand. pH sustainability is still low, like gravel. Perlite does not degrade over time, but it's generally not reused because it's difficult to clean. Perlite comes in many sizes, but the larger ½-inch to 1-inch sizes lend themselves to hydroponic applications best.

COMPATIBLE SYSTEMS
Subirrigation

Rock Wool

Rock wool is available in many forms, but must always be kept covered to keep mold and mildew at bay.

Developed by the Grodan Company in 1969, rock wool is made from natural rocks melted down and blown into mineral fibers in a process that is similar to the way fiberglass insulation is made. This layering process gives rock wool the unparalleled water-to-air ratio of up to 94 percent. That's an almost equal amount of water to air in the state of resting saturation. Water retention is good and its extreme porosity makes it drain well.

The type of rocks used in the manufacturing process cause the initial pH of rock wool to be around 7.7 to 8.0, too alkaline for plants. Use a solution with a pH of 5.5 to 5.8 to soak the rock wool and bring the pH into optimum range. Commercial conditioners or lemon juice can also be used. Rock wool's pH sustainability is good, but unfortunately rock wool has a tendency to hold its initial pH. Nutrient retention is also good, so many companies now produce rock wool–specific conditioner formulas that hold the pH in range. These conditioners and nutrient solutions are synthetic, so rock wool culture is usually not considered organic, but using lemon juice and organic nutrients is possible with close pH monitoring. For the best results, to feed plants, use synthetic nutrient solutions specifically formulated for use with rock wool.

Rock wool comes in a variety of sizes, plugs, and mats for propagation; cubes for small- to medium-sized plants; and slabs that these cubes can be placed on top of—mimicking transplanting.

The alkaline nature and porosity of rock wool makes it subject to aggressive growth of green algae, molds, and mildews. Always keep the rock wool enclosed or covered so light cannot reach it or these will become problematic.

COMPATIBLE SYSTEMS
Subirrigation
Timed-drip systems
Covered systems

Expanded Clay Pellets (Hydroton)

Expanded clay pellets are made from blends of different clays fired in an open furnace to eliminate heavy metals and other contaminants. This process produces a light, porous, clay ball that's 8 millimeters to 16 millimeters in size with an irregular shape, good water retention, and a pH sustainability that guards against excess acidity. Systems using expanded clay pellets have few insect problems, generally, but green algae will grow on its surface. This media has a neutral pH of 7 and has good nutrient retention, making it an ideal aggregate. Expanded clay pellets have all of the beneficial properties of gravel and perlite combined. Organic and reusable, expanded clay pellets are popular among both professionals and enthusiasts.

Clay pellets are expensive but reusable.

COMPATIBLE SYSTEMS
Subirrigation
Constant and timed-drip systems

Coco Coir

Coco coir is a relatively new type of media. It's manufactured using the fibers from the husks of coconuts. There's no standard way to manufacture coco coir, so the contents of a package of this media can vary by producer. Generally, the woody inside of a husk is used. It is removed from the coconut by machines that carve, shred, or chunk it up into small pieces. Manufacturers use any number of processes to finish it, from washing to remove excess EC; buffering to remove excess potassium; pasteurizing to kill weeds, seeds, and bacteria; and then sieving to remove foreign material and increase uniformity.

Coir, a coconut plant byproduct, is a renewable resource.

The water-to-air ratio of coco coir is good. Water retention is high; coco coir holds water for quite a while so systems can go longer between watering, similar to soil. Initial pH is usually neutral (7), but always check. Coco coir's pH sustainability is very good, as is nutrient retention because of coco coir's slower drainage and drying rate. Special nutrient blends exist specifically tailored to coco to optimize its special properties. Although any nutrient solution can be used, organic or synthetic, the solutions specifically tailored to use with coco coir are recommended. Coco coir is susceptible to insect infestations, as well as algae and fungal problems.

COMPATIBLE SYSTEMS
Hand-watering
Timed-drip

Compressed Bark
Compressed bark is made of composted tree bark and select organic material that's inoculated with beneficial microbes and pressed into mats or plugs. These mats or plugs are great for germinating seeds and propagating cuttings. The water-to-air ratio and water retention in this media are better suited for healthy root development than soil. Compressed bark is organic, with a neutral ph. The pH sustainability is similar to soil. Microbiology does well in this medium (it functions similar to soil), so nutrient retention is on par with soil—not just holding nutrients but functioning as a successful host for microbes that produce nutrients and facilitate nutrient uptake. Compressed bark is considered by most to be the premier medium for propagation and germination, as well as a more organic alternative to rock wool or low-density foam, although it is not OMRI listed.

COMPATIBLE SYSTEMS
Propagation systems
Cloning trays

These types of plugs can be cut in half to save on overhead costs.

Low-Density High-Drainage Foam

Developed for plants that require a high water usage, low-density high-drainage foam is now being used as a propagation and germination medium. It is firmer than rock wool, but with a similar high level of porosity, offering an optimal balance of air and water for early root development, with exceptional drainage. It is inorganic, has a neutral pH7, and exhibits good nutrient sustainability and retention.

COMPATIBLE SYSTEMS
Propagation systems

An aerocloner with neoprene inserts holds stem cuttings.

Soilless Pro-Mix

Some professionals and enthusiasts have started experimenting with mixing their own media to get the specific result they desire, in terms of pH, water-to-air ratio, water retention, and so forth. In addition to all the previously listed media, Canadian sphagnum peat moss, organic polymers, chemical wetting agents, dolomite or calcitic limestone, gypsum, and vermiculite can all be used to amend growing media properties or to create a custom mix.

Canadian sphagnum peat moss is usually used as a base in the mix as a more porous alternative to coco coir. Organic polymers and wetting agents are added to increase water and nutrient retention, making the need for irrigation less frequent. Adding limestone adjusts pH, bringing it into the desirable range. Vermiculite is used to increase nutrient and water retention. Rock wool can be added for its capillary properties. Gravel, perlite, or hydroton are used to improve drainage, increasing the water-to-air ratio and increasing irrigation frequency needs. Propagation media such as compressed bark can be chunked up and mixed in to add inoculants, promoting beneficial microbiology.

COMPATIBLE SYSTEMS

These mixes can be custom tailored to fit almost any feeding schedule and irrigation technique, and are an inventive solution to problems like leaching, over-drainage, undesirable water retention, initial pH issues, and low porosity.

Drip system:
- 30% Canadian sphagnum peat moss
- 20% Hydroton or gravel
- 20% Course perlite
- 10% Coco coir
- 10% Vermiculite
- 5% Chunked compressed bark (inoculated)
- 5% Dolomite limestone

Subirrigation:
- 60% Hydroton or gravel
- 20% Coarse perlite
- 15% Vermiculite
- 5% Chunked compressed bark (inoculated)

When mixing your own growing media, think in terms of *parts*, with the whole consisting of twenty parts. Use a kiddie pool or a 54-gallon tote and a 1-gallon container to measure out your ingredients. Mix well for a steady, consistent result, or layer each ingredient in individual containers for specific effects. For example: hydroton at the bottom for drainage purposes, the mix layered over that, and hydroton at the top to act as mulch.

WATER CULTURE

Water culture is the practice of using *no* growing media at all. Plants are held in place in the container using a cork or neoprene insert. Roots are allowed to dangle directly into a nutrient solution, or are sprayed constantly or in intervals.

The nutrient solution needs to be circulated to prevent localized depletion of nutrients, and it must be aerated to oxygenate the solution. Even though no medium is being used, air is present, giving water culture a unique set of challenges, different from cultures involving growing media.

Water is not, technically, considered a growing media, but it does share some characteristics of growing media. Water-to-air ratio is achieved with an air pump. Water retention is nonexistent (plants are either in air being sprayed with nutrient solution or completely submersed in water). Initial pH is the nutrient solution's pH, and since pH changes during the feeding cycle, and pH sustainability is nonexistent without growing media, careful monitoring of the

pH or automated adjustment methods must be employed. Essentially all the protective buffering and retaining properties of a medium are gone, which means any problems with irrigation quickly escalate.

The tradeoff is unparalleled feeding potential with the direct delivery of a highly oxygenated nutrient solution to the root zone and an almost immediate initiation of the drying cycle when feeding (and watering) ceases. When constant feeding is used, a portion of the root zone is usually kept dry to facilitate a good mix of wet and dry roots. Deep water culture (DWC) was the first water culture irrigation technique developed, and it remains in use today. The nutrient film technique (NFT) is another water culture technique that is much more practical for large-scale horticultural/agricultural applications than for cannabis production. The most effective irrigation technique developed for water culture is the aeroponic irrigation technique.

Each of these growing media is compatible with different types of watering systems. The next chapter describes the systems and how the medium is incorporated into the system.

Hydroton's shape and porous nature make it ideal for hydroponics. Its round shape allows plant roots to grow more easily, with less stress, as they can grow around the clay balls, and it absorbs both water and nutrients.

CHAPTER 5

Watering Systems

If you're growing marijuana at home, you're going to use one of the following types of systems to deliver water and nutrients to the plants.

- Hand-watering
- Drip irrigation
- Wick technique
- Deep water culture
- Subirrigation (flood and drain)
- Gutter systems
- Drip gutter

Each system has its pros and cons. Some are better suited to smaller operations, while others will allow you to grow more plants at a time. A few of the systems require external power and pumps, while others work entirely with elbow grease and gravity. You'll select the preferred watering technique based on the amount of product you want to grow and harvest, the type of growing medium used (if any), and the availability of electrical power.

Though growing media are described in a separate chapter, growing media and watering systems do relate to one another. The ideal types of growing media are noted with each watering system.

Opposite: Whether you're hand-watering or building an intricate hydroponic watering system, delivering a consistent supply of water and food to your plants is critical. This chapter presents and discusses seven systems that will work in just about any home-growing environment.

WATERING SYSTEMS FOR HOME GROWERS

Hand-Watering (See page 67)

Hand watering is the simplest method (or, at least the easiest to set up). It is mostly used when plants are grown on a small scale or for demonstration purposes. The nutrient solution is poured over the medium, usually sand, and allowed to percolate down through the container. The excess solution then drains off with the use of a valve or by gravity alone. You can reuse the nutrient solution as long as it still contains the correct pH and nutrient content. This technique is useful in the event of equipment failure when using other techniques.

Best for: Small-scale and demonstration systems
Compatible growing media: Sand, cocoa mulch, Pro-Mix
Electrical power needed: No
Growth stage: Any

Drip Irrigation (See page 71)

This technique is popular with professionals and enthusiasts alike. Drip irrigation is suitable for any size garden, from huge commercial endeavors to a single plant.

Best for: All sizes of gardens
Compatible growing media: All
Electrical power needed: Yes
Growth stage: Any

Auto-Irrigating Wick Technique (See page 75)

A wick system is an auto-irrigating technique that works best when used with larger sand particles for the growing medium. This is a less maintenance-intensive system than some and can go for 3 days or so without intervention.

Best for: Single plants, demonstration systems
Compatible growing medium: Sand
Electrical power needed: no
Growth stage: Any

Deep Water Culture (See page 79)

This technique allows roots to grow directly in the nutrient solution. You can make one for single-plant or multiple-site (multiple plants) systems, provided that the nutrient solution is distributed equally to all plants.

Best for: At-home growers with single-bucket systems

Compatible growing media: No medium—uses neoprene inserts

Electrical power needed: Yes

Growth stage: Plants with a life cycle 18 weeks or less

Subirrigation (Flood and Drain) (See page 87)

Subirrigation is the technique of feeding plants from below (sub). The nutrient solution is pumped from a well-oxygenated reservoir into the growing tray that holds the individual plants.

Best for: Closets, open rooms, or growers who need a more automated system

Compatible growing media: All, but rock wool or coco coir will require longer drying periods between feedings than expanded clay pellets or gravel.

Electrical power needed: Yes

Growth stage: Any, but take into consideration plant size, water retention, water-to-air ratio, and nutrient retention when calculating a feeding schedule

Gutter (See page 89)

Gutter systems use enclosed or open 6 × 6 inch or larger plastic rain gutters as planters. This type of system can accommodate a varied number and arrangement of planting sites and a variety of irrigation techniques.

Best for: Any size system

Compatible growing media: All, but lighter, faster-draining media, such as perlite or coir, work better than heaver materials, such as sand

Electrical power needed: Yes

Growth stage: Any

Drip Gutter (See page 92)

This irrigation system is easy to construct and maintain. It delivers water directly to each plant by use of a stake and drippers or emitters.

Best for: Gardens with 12 or more plants

Compatible growing media: All growing media; rock wool in a sleeve works well for open gutter systems

Electrical power needed: Yes

Growth stage: Any

The hand-watering system is as simple as it gets.

HAND-WATERING

This is mostly used when plants are grown on a small scale or for demonstration purposes. The nutrient solution is poured over the medium, usually sand, and allowed to percolate down through the container. The excess solution then drains off into an empty bucket with the use of a valve or by gravity alone. You can reuse the nutrient solution as long as it still contains the correct pH and nutrient content. This technique is useful in the event of equipment failure when using other techniques.

Best for: Small-scale and demonstration systems
Compatible growing medium: Sand, cocoa mulch, Pro-Mix
Electrical power needed: No
Growth stage: All

MATERIALS

A Bucket or drainage reservoir for each growing container/tub (such as an empty, clean, 1-gallon milk jug)
B Cordless drill and bits
C Growing medium
D Plants
E Pots (6-inch)
F, G Plastic adhesive or bulkhead fitting
H Growing tray (4-inch-deep tub or tray)
I Wood block (to create incline)
J Plastic tubing
K Table or elevated supports

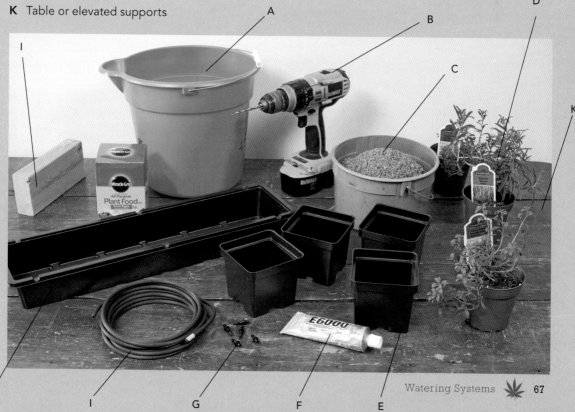

HOW TO BUILD A HAND-WATERING SYSTEM

1. In a corner of the tray, drill a drainage hole in the bottom of the growing tray. (If you want to reuse the tray, cut the hole so that it can easily be plugged with a 1-inch rubber stopper.)

2. Fill the pots with growing medium, then plant the plants.

3. Secure the drain tube in the drain hole using strong plastic adhesive if necessary. Or install a bulkhead fitting. Place the fitting in the hole with the rubber seal on the inside of the tray. Tighten the locknut from below. Attach the plastic tubing to the nipple of the fitting. These are usually barbed fittings, so simply push into place.

4. Position the tray on a table or supports so that the drain hole clears the edge of the table or supports. Place the pots in the growing tub.

5. Place the reservoir on the floor, and line up the tub so that the drainage tube runs directly down into the reservoir bucket.

6. Insert the wood block under the end of the tub opposite the drainage hole to create an incline. Or you can place the block under a leg of the table or support. As long as the far side (the side away from the drainage hole) is elevated, the solution will drain into the reservoir. The incline only needs to be ¼ to ½ inch per foot for effective draining. With a larger incline, the individual pots will slide around.

HOW TO USE A HAND-WATERING SYSTEM

1. Pour the nutrient solution over the growing medium, starting with the pots at the elevated end of the container. Pour enough solution over the plants so that the medium and plant roots are thoroughly moistened. Water gently so that you do not damage the roots of the plants or erode the medium.

2. Allow the solution to run out and collect in the reservoir. Test the pH and nutrient content of the nutrient solution before reusing it.

3. Water again when the growing medium is dry. Resist the urge to water too frequently—before the medium has had a chance to dry out—because this can cause root rot. Water again when the medium contains 12 percent moisture or less. If the plants are wilting between watering, you are waiting too long between watering. How do you know the soil is at 12 percent moisture content? The top of the medium will be dry with only a trace of moisture near the bottom of the pot. Or, you can use a moisture meter.

DRIP IRRIGATION

This technique is popular with professionals and enthusiasts alike. Drip irrigation is suitable for any size garden, from huge commercial endeavors to a single plant, which is the setup shown here. In this version, a submersible pump placed in the bottom of a 5-gallon bucket moves the nutrient solution up an irrigation line. Spaghetti tubing, which is ¼-inch tubing, connects to the main line. An emitter or 1- to 5-gallon-per-hour (GPH) dripper that is connected to the spaghetti tubing provides the feeding solution to the plant. Most of these components—except for the pump—are part of most drip irrigation kits. The unused solution seeps out of the bottom of the pot and returns to the bucket. Feeding frequency depends on the water retention properties of your medium and the specific needs of your plants. The frequency ranges from a constant flow to feeding for 15 minutes every 3 to 4 hours.

Best for: All sizes of gardens
Compatible growing medium: All
Electrical power needed: Yes
Growth stage: Any

MATERIALS

A 5-gallon bucket with a lid
B 6-inch pot for planting
C Utility knife or hole saw attachment for a drill
D Cordless drill
E Submersible pump (160 GPH) with barbed fittings
F 3 feet of polytube (polyethylene irrigation tubing) that fits the pump, with plug or line clamp
G Spaghetti tube and hole punch
H Growing medium
I Drip emitter or a stake and dripper

A drip-irrigation system supplies a continuous, low volume flow of water/nutrient solution to the plant via a pump, tubing and an emitter. This simple version is made with a 5-gallon bucket and easily supports one adult plant.

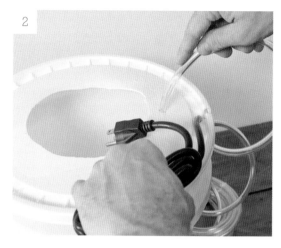

1. Trace the bottom diameter of the pot on the bucket lid. The bottom of the pot should be slightly smaller than the top. Use the utility knife or hole saw attachment to cut a hole in the bucket lid. Place the pot in the hole to make sure it fits snugly. The lip of the pot should support it in the hole.

2. Drill a 1-inch-diameter hole in the bucket lid (next to the hole you drilled for the plant pot). Drill another hole near the edge of the lid. Place the pump in the bottom of the bucket. Connect the polytube to the barbed head on the submersible pump. Thread the tubing through the hole near the plant pot hole. Run the pump's power cord through the other hole.

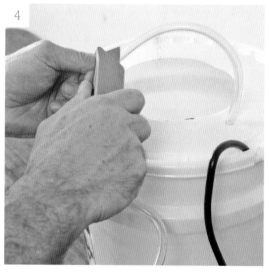

3. Add 2 gallons of nutrient solution to the bucket, and put the lid in place.

4. Cut the end of the tubing, leaving 4 to 6 inches above the lid of the bucket.

5. Using the spaghetti tube hole-punch, punch a hole 1 to 2 inches from the end of the polytube irrigation line.

6. Connect the spaghetti tube to the irrigation tubing with a barbed coupling or nipple.

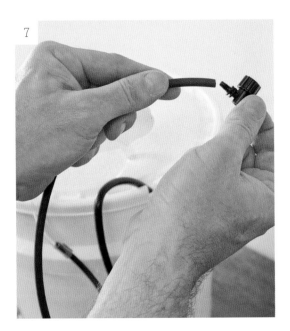

7. Connect the stake and dripper or emitter to the other end of the spaghetti tube. Plug the top end of the tube so that the line will pressurize. You can also double back the line on itself and clamp it.

8. Plant the plant, and place it in the hole in the lid. Place the emitter next to the plant. Plug in the pump's power cord to start the flow of the solution. Remember to change the nutrient solution every 7 to 10 days for salt-based synthetic solutions and every 5 to 7 days for organic solutions.

AUTO-IRRIGATING WICK TECHNIQUE

This system consists of two buckets—one bucket is nested inside the other. A porous, natural-fiber wick runs from the bottom bucket through the top bucket. The capillary effect of the porous wick draws the nutrient solution upward from the reservoir to the root zone of the plant, providing water and nutrients. The auto-irrigating technique works best when used with larger sand particles for the growing medium. This is a less maintenance-intensive system than some and can go for 3 days or so without intervention.

Best for: Single plants, demonstration systems
Compatible growing medium: Sand
Electrical power needed: No
Growth stage: All

MATERIALS

A Sand
B Two 5-gallon buckets
C Plants
D Cordless drill and bits
E Wicking cord (hemp, cotton, jute rope)
F Utility knife
G Nutrient solution

HOW TO BUILD THE AUTO-IRRIGATING WICK TECHNIQUE SYSTEM

1. Drill a hole slightly smaller than the diameter of the wicking material in the bottom of what will be the top bucket. Thread the wick through the hole. Make sure the wick is long enough to run from the bottom of the bottom bucket to the top of the top bucket when the buckets are stacked. Add 1 to 2 gallons of nutrient solution to the bottom bucket.

2. Place the top bucket into the bottom bucket with the wick in place.

3. Fill the top bucket with sand, leaving 3 inches between the top of the sand and the top of the bucket. Plant the plant, making sure the wick is slightly off center as it passes by the root zone.

HOW TO USE THE AUTO-IRRIGATING WICK TECHNIQUE SYSTEM

1. Check the system at least every 3 days to make sure that the wick is working properly and nutrient solution is reaching the plants. (If you see signs of wilting plants or nutrient deficiencies, the plants are not getting the water at the root zone.)

2. Flush the medium with clean water every 14 to 20 days. You can use regular water, reverse osmosis filtered water, or UV sterilized water. Do **not** use distilled water. To flush, remove the top bucket, and empty the lower bucket. Replace the top bucket, and slowly pour clean water over the sand so that it drains into the lower bucket. Discard the clean water, repeat, and add fresh nutrient solution to the bottom bucket.

DEEP WATER CULTURE

This technique allows roots to grow directly in the nutrient solution. Oxygenation of the solution is key to success. In a multiple-site (multiple plants) system, circulation of the solution is necessary to avoid a localized depletion of nutrients.

Best for: At-home growers with single-bucket systems
Compatible growing media: No medium—uses neoprene inserts
Electrical power needed: Yes
Growth stage: Plants with a life cycle 18 weeks or less

MATERIALS

A 5-gallon bucket with a lid
B Cordless drill and bits
C, F Air-line tubing and an air stone (the larger the stone, the better)
D Utility knife or 4-inch hole saw attachment for a drill
E 4-inch neoprene insert for each plant/bucket
G Air pump (1.3 liters per minute minimum)
H Plants

1. Use the neoprene insert as a template to mark the hole in the center of the lid. Use the utility knife or hole saw to cut out the hole.

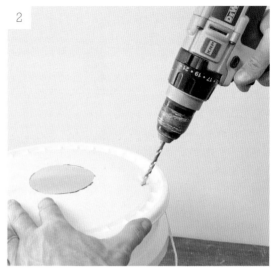

2. Drill the hole for the air-line tube near the edge of the bucket lid. (This will normally be a ¼-inch hole for standard tubing.)

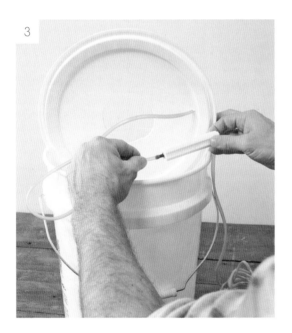

3. Feed the air-line tubing through the hole in the lid, and connect the tubing to the air stone. Place the air stone in the bottom of the bucket.

4. Fill the bucket with nutrient solution up to a level where 60 to 80 percent of the roots will be submerged once the lid is put in place.

5. Secure the lid on top of the bucket, and push the free end of the air line onto the air pump's outlet nipple. Plug in the air pump.

6. Insert the plant into the neoprene insert, and place the insert into the hole in the bucket lid. The plant roots should be immersed in the solution. Add solution as necessary.

TIP: You can fabricate a multi-site deep water culture system by using a large, plastic tote. (Totes come in several different sizes; choose the one that best accommodates the number of plants you want to include.) Drill or cut multiple holes in the lid, and place more than one air stone in the reservoir to achieve the proper level of oxygenation. (See page 42; proper oxygenation looks like a carbonated beverage.) A submersible pump can be used to circulate the solution. Just place it in the tote, and run the power cord out through a hole in the lid. The pump will churn the water, mixing it so that the nutrients are spread evenly throughout the solution. In this system, the submersible pump circulates the solution and is used in concert with the air pumps.

HOW TO USE THE DEEP WATER CULTURE SYSTEM
Change the nutrient solution every 7 to 10 days for salt-based synthetic solutions, and every 5 to 7 days for organic solutions. Run the air stone continuously.

RESERVOIR SYSTEMS

Larger irrigation systems—those that service multiple plants—require some sort of container or tank to hold nutrient solutions in between feeding cycles. In these systems, the solution is pumped to the plants, and the runoff is directed back to the reservoir to be recycled. Flood and drain systems, gutter systems, and drip gutter systems require a reservoir. Instructions for building a reservoir system are below, followed by instructions for building larger watering systems that require a reservoir. Most of the supplies needed to construct a reservoir are available at aquarium stores, garden centers that sell hydroponic equipment, and online.

Best for: Open rooms and multiple plants
Compatible growing media: No medium—uses neoprene inserts
Electrical power needed: Yes
Growth stage: Any, but varies with demands of number and stage of plants

MATERIALS

A One 54-gallon plastic tote with a lid
B Cordless drill and bits
C Air pump (1.3 liters per minute minimum)
D Air stone (the larger the better)
E Nutrient solution
F Submersible aquarium heater
G Floating aquarium thermometer
H Submersible water pump (160 GPH minimum)
I Air-line tubing

HOW TO BUILD THE RESERVOIR SYSTEM

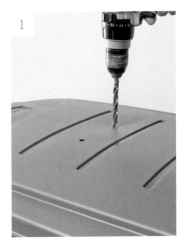

1. Drill two holes in the container lid for the polytubing. One is for tubing that connects to the circulation pump, and the other is for the solution to return back to the reservoir. The holes should be about 4 inches apart.

2. Drill a large hole on the opposite side of the lid for the pump's and heater's electrical cords, and the air-line tube. The hole should be big enough for the plugs to pass through.

3. Place the air stone in the container. Connect the air pump and air stone. This is usually a direct connection with the tube running from the pump outlet to the air stone inlet nipple.

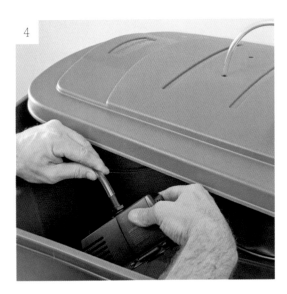

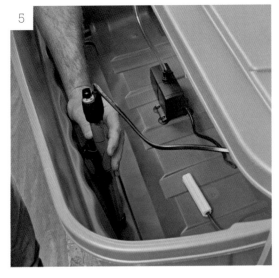

4. Place the submersible pump in the container. Connect the polytubing to the pump, and thread the tubing through one of the holes in the lid. The length of the tubing will depend on which watering system you are attaching the reservoir to and the distance between the reservoir and the plants.

5. Fill the reservoir container with 30 gallons of nutrient solution and place the aquarium heater and the floating thermometer in the container. Heaters usually hang over the side or can be attached to the walls of the container with suction cups.

HOW TO USE THE RESERVOIR SYSTEM

At this point the reservoir is ready to be used with one of the irrigation systems described below. The only change you will need to make is in the way the run-off is returned to the reservoir, which is described with each of the systems.

The reservoir can be either covered or uncovered. If using an uncovered reservoir, expect some evaporation of the solution as well as a rise in the relative humidity (RH) of the growing room. If the RH goes above 60 percent, you will need to lower it by cooling the area or the use of dehumidifiers. See Chapter 6 for more on growing room environments.

When ready, plug in the air and water pumps, and the heater. Before plugging in the aquarium heater, allow the heater to become acclimated to the temperature of the water. This usually takes about 30 minutes, but follow the manufacturer's directions. If you plug everything into a surge protector, you can control the equipment with a flick of a switch.

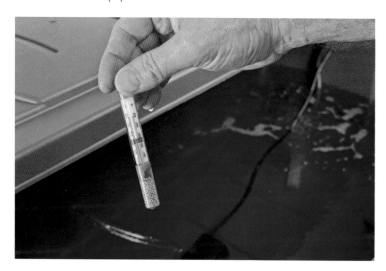

Nutrient solution in the reservoir will need to be checked and changed on a regular basis. Check the temperature and chemical levels every 72 hours and run the air stone continuously. See page 123 for nutrient solution information. The fluid in these types of reservoirs should be changed every 7 to 10 days for salt-based synthetic solutions, and every 5 to 7 days for organic solutions. (You can use the old nutrient solution to water indoor and outdoor plants, as well as vegetables in the garden.)

To empty the reservoir and change the solution, pump the water out using the submersible pump until the weight of the container is easily managed, and it can be lifted by hand. You can disconnect electrical connections or, if the cords are long enough, shut off power and remove the lid with the cords in place.

SUBIRRIGATION (FLOOD AND DRAIN)

Subirrigation is the technique of feeding plants from below (sub). The nutrient solution is pumped from a well-oxygenated reservoir into the growing tray that holds the individual plants. The solution floods the roots of the plants. An overflow tube keeps the solution from rising too high and overflowing the growing tray. At the end of the feeding cycle, the pump is switched off, and the solution drains back to the reservoir. Use automatic timers to reduce the work you'll have to do and keep feeding schedules consistent.

Best for: Closets, open rooms, or growers who need a more automated system
Compatible growing media: All, but rock wool or coco coir will require longer drying periods between feedings than expanded clay pellets or gravel will
Electrical power needed: Yes
Growth stage: All, but take into consideration plant size, water retention, water-to-air ratio, and nutrient retention when calculating a feeding schedule

MATERIALS

A Polytube that fits the drain nipple of the flood and drain kit
B Plastic container (grow tray) at least 7 inches high and the desired length and width
C Reservoir (See page 84 for instructions on how to build a reservoir.)
D Flood and drain kit (sometimes called ebb and flow kit, available where hydroponic equipment is sold or online)
E Aquarium pump
F Timer
G Cordless drill and hole saw attachments
H Growing medium

TIP: Two 17-liter totes can be fed at the same time from one 45-gallon (or larger) reservoir by putting a T connector on the "flood" line (the line running from the pump to the planters). Polytube fittings usually have barbed connections, but you should ensure against leaks by installing hose clamps as well.

BUILD THE SUBIRRIGATION SYSTEM

1. Cut two holes in the bottom of the tray about 4 inches apart to accommodate the flood and drain fittings.

3. Place the growing tray on the sawhorses or the growing tray supports.

2. Adjust the fittings to the desired height. The flood fitting, where the solution enters the tub, should be as low as possible. The drain fitting should be about 1 inch below the top surface of the growing medium.

4. Place the fittings in the holes. The fittings come with rubber seals. If there is one seal, place it under the fitting's flange on the inside of the tray. If there are two seals, place one inside and one on the outside of the growing tray. Tighten the fittings' locknuts from below.

5. Connect the polytube that is connected to the pump in the reservoir to the flood fitting. These are usually barbed fittings so simply push the tubing into place. Run polytubing from the drain fitting to the reservoir. (The drain fitting may be larger than the fill fitting, so you will need larger polytube for the drain.)

6. Fill the plastic mesh pots with growing medium and plant the plants.

7. Set the pots in the growing tray. You can place them on the floor of the tray, or if the tray comes with a lid with cutouts for the pots, place the pots in the holes.

HOW TO USE THE SUBIRRIGATION SYSTEM

A typical feeding schedule would be 15 minutes feeding, 45 minutes off, for the first half of the plant's life. Then increase to 30 minutes feeding, 30 minutes off, as the plant gets larger. Set the timer to the feeding schedule. Check the system every 3 or 4 days to ensure that it is working properly. The fluid in these types of reservoirs should be changed every 7 to 10 days for salt-based synthetic solutions, and every 5 to 7 days for organic solutions.

GUTTER SYSTEMS

Gutter systems use enclosed or open 6×6 inch or larger plastic rain gutters as planters. If you have trouble finding 6-inch gutters, use the largest size you can find. You can also use downspouts for this growing technique. This type of system can accommodate a varied number and arrangement of planting sites and a variety of irrigation techniques. One reservoir can water several planting sites at the same time with only one submersible pump and some creative use of space. The gutters should sit on an angle to facilitate drainage.

- **Best for:** Any-size system
- **Compatible growing media:** All, but lighter, faster-draining media, such as perlite or coir, work better than heaver materials, such as sand
- **Electrical power needed:** Yes
- **Growth stage:** All

MATERIALS

A Planting pots

B Gutter (with leaf guard or other enclosure, or a completely open version); 1 foot of gutter length per plant is the minimum to finish clones flowered directly after rooting; 3 feet per plant with vegetation period of 2 weeks or more (see "Life Cycle" on page 19)

C Growing media

D Tubing clamps or zip ties

E PVC bulkhead fitting with barbed connection

F Reservoir assembly (see "How to Build a Reservoir" on page 84)

G Aquarium pump

H Cordless drill and 4-inch and 1-inch hole saw attachments

I Wood block (to create incline)

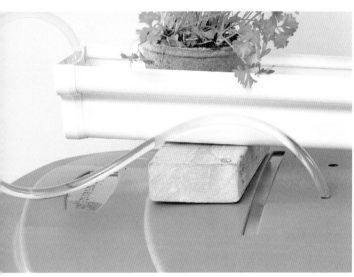

HOW TO BUILD THE GUTTER SYSTEM

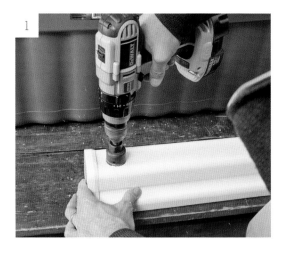

1. Use the 1-inch hole saw to create an opening for the bulkhead fitting at one end of the gutter. Use a 4-inch hole saw to open planting sites (in covered gutters), or pot up plants in containers of desired size for open gutters (4-inch pots work well in open gutters).

2. Install the fitting using the supplied rubber seals and tightening the lock nut from below.

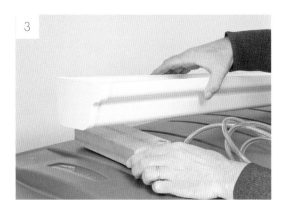

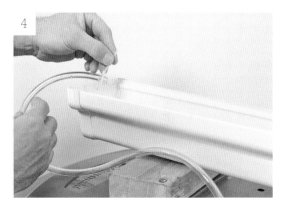

3. Set the gutter on the tables or sawhorses with the end opposite the drain tube raised about ¼ inch per 1 foot of gutter. It is important to angle the gutter down toward the reservoir at a 6-degree or more severe angle.

4. Run the polytube from the pump in the reservoir to the high end of the gutter. If necessary, use zip ties to hold it in place. Connect the polytube drainage line to the drainage fitting, and run it back to the reservoir.

HOW TO USE THE GUTTER SYSTEM

Change the nutrient solution every 7 to 10 days for salt-based synthetic solutions, and every 5 to 7 days for organic solutions.

Set the timer so that the system runs for the specified amount of time. A typical feeding schedule would be 15 minutes feeding, 45 minutes off for the first half of the plant's life, or 30 minutes on 30 minutes off for larger plants or any that are wilting between feedings. Check the system and the plants every 3 or 4 days.

DRIP GUTTER

An improvement on the single-site drip technique (drip buckets), this irrigation system is easy to construct and maintain. This system delivers water directly to each plant by use of a stake and drippers or emitters.

Best for: Gardens with 12 or more plants
Compatible growing media: All growing media; rock wool in a sleeve works well for open gutter systems
Electrical power needed: Yes
Growth stage: Any

MATERIALS

A Gutter system
B Neoprene inserts (for closed gutters) or 4-inch pots or rock wool sleeves (for open gutters)
C Reservoir (See page 84)
D Aquarium pump
E Drill and bits
F Tubing hole punch
G Growing medium (if using pots)
H Wood block
I Spaghetti tubing
J Irrigation polytubing
K Tubing clamps or zip ties
L Tables or sawhorses

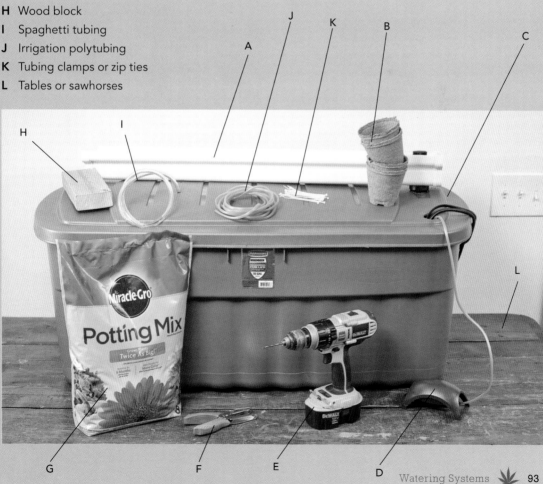

HOW TO BUILD THE DEEP GUTTER SYSTEM

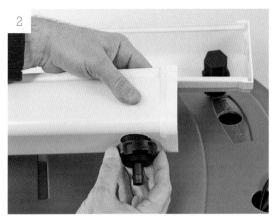

1. Construct a reservoir system as described on page 84.

2. Construct a gutter system as described on page 91, using multiple gutters. Drill drainage holes through one end of the gutters.

3. Set up the gutters on tables, sawhorses, or other supports, and angle them so that they drain about ¼ inch for every foot of gutter. Use wood blocks to raise individual gutters, or raise the entire table. The drainage holes in the gutters should overlap the edge of an uncovered reservoir.

5. Keep the tubing in place using tubing clamps or zip ties.

4. For open gutters, line each gutter with polytubing. For closed gutters, place the tubing on top. For multiple gutters, run the tubing up one gutter and down the next and so on. To make turns, use poly elbows. The connections have barbed fittings, but use hose clamps where the tubing connects to the fittings to ensure against leaks.

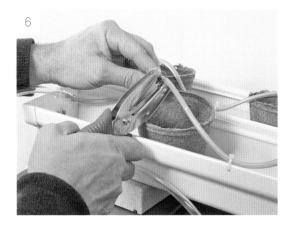

6. Using the hole punch, cut into the tubing where the plants will be placed: for clones that flowered directly after rooting, cut 1 foot per plant (minimum); for plants with a veg period of 2 weeks or more, cut every 3 feet per plant.

7. Attach spaghetti tubing using barbed connectors, and run tubing to the plant sites.

8. Place the pots, fill with a medium or place rock wool blocks or mats, and plant the plants.

9. Install emitters on the tubing, and place them in position in the pots.

TIP: Rock wool works well as a planting medium for open-gutter systems. Rock wool is purchased in 4-inch or larger cubes, or as a plastic-enclosed mat. Use rock wool blocks for early plant life or plant directly into the mat.

HOW TO USE THE DEEP GUTTER SYSTEM

This system works well when the medium is allowed to dry out between watering. You have to experiment with watering and dry periods if you are using a timer. Soak the medium, and then time how long it takes to dry out. Use the information to set an automatic timer.

Change the nutrient solution every 7 to 10 days for salt-based synthetic solutions, and every 5 to 7 days for organic solutions.

CHAPTER 6

The Growing Environment

To grow marijuana plants indoors successfully, you need to create the growing environment that meets the plants' needs. That means balancing a number of conflicting environmental factors. For example, the artificial lights the plants need to thrive produce enough heat to damage or kill the plants. To correct the imbalance, the area needs to be cooled and the heat removed through a ventilation system. The growing environment is the infrastructure surrounding the plants—where the watering system, lights, fans, carbon dioxide (CO_2) enhancement, and so forth run. This chapter will show ways to provide a successful growing environment. It will show how to build growing chambers and how to choose and construct the best circulation system for your plants.

Above: Unplugging your dryer and installing a light box can be a quick alternative.

Opposite: Growing marijuana indoors allows you to control these critical factors: light cycles, temperature, and ventilation.

KNOW BEFORE YOU GROW

Before you can build your indoor garden, you need to examine electrical requirements for the system(s) you plan to build and, if necessary, upgrade the electrical service. In most cases, modifications to your home's electrical system will require a licensed electrician to ensure the changes are done correctly and to code.

First, check your home's circuit box. There should be a map or at least a list of the areas served by each breaker or fuse. The growing environment will need two different circuits, If you plan on converting an existing living space to a growing environment, you will need to be wise about your choice equipement. Two 12-amp circuits in a house can run a light and environmental controls for a 4x4 foot area, or a 4x8 foot area with a light rail. Larger gardens with multiple lights will require umplugging your dryer and hooking up a lightbox off the 30-amp usually there or calling an electrician to upgrade your home's existing circuit box.

If the circuit box does not have a map, you can make your own. You can map it yourself by plugging a voltage tester into an outlet. Flip the breakers on and off until you find the one that turns the light on the tester off. That is the breaker that corresponds to the outlet where the tester is plugged in. Note which outlet in the room goes with each breaker as you move through the process. Some outlets or individual receptacles may be connected to a three-way switch in the room. Always check the switches in both positions when testing your electrical outlets. (Note: Testers are available for $10 or less. A multi-meter, or multi-tester, is more sophisticated, and more expensive, than a simple voltage tester, but it too can help map circuits. Anyone who doesn't feel absolutely confident in their abilities to deal with electrical circuits and wiring should hire a licensed electrician.)

Don't overload your circuits. Pulling 75 percent of available amps per circuit is considered the ceiling for safe operation (18.75 amps of power pulled from a 25-amp breaker). As part of your safety plan, consider installing automatic self-contained ABC-rated fire extinguishers. They provide protection from all sorts of fires, including electrical fires. Just hang them over outlets and lamp sites. They are triggered by a temperature probe and dispense a multipurpose dry chemical extinguisher. Complement the fire extinguishers by installing smoke detectors in the growing area. Follow these safety considerations, and you will be a responsible and safe indoor gardening enthusiast.

PREPARING AND CREATING THE GROW ROOM

The key to creating a successful indoor gardening environment is control, which means managing all of the environmental conditions detailed in Chapter 3. By controlling the environmental conditions, you'll provide ideal growing conditions and be better able to prevent pest infestations and growth of molds, fungi, and bacteria.

You gain control over the growing environment by creating smaller, more manageable areas inside a larger environment. The larger environment is called the "grow room." Within the grow room are smaller chambers where you can control the growing conditions. Think of the grow room as a buffer between the outside world and the growing chambers from bugs, molds, and fungal spores as well as cold, heat, and humidity.

The location of the grow room will depend on what is available in your home. It could be a corner of a basement, a garage, or shed—as long as there is electrical power and running water available—or a little-used room in the house. The important point is that the grow room needs to be separated from the living areas of the house.

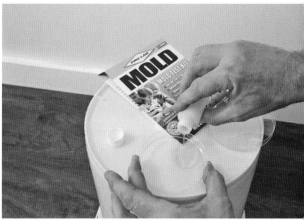

Step 1: Strip down the room

It is important to create a clean, pest-free environment, so begin by removing things like carpet and wallpaper. They can harbor unwanted moisture and spores that can cause mold and fungal problems. Once you have the room stripped bare, clean it with an organic cleaner like BioGreen Clean or any of the Everest Nation products. These products are nontoxic to humans and kill any mold spores or fungi present that can't be seen with the naked eye. (Note: The biggest entry point for mold is via walls, specifically interior walls that contain plumbing runs. To be extra cautious, you can purchase a mold test from a home-improvement store.) Once the room is clean, make it a point to keep it that way. Always pick up after yourself before leaving, clean up any spills, and make sure everything is in order.

Above left: Prevention is the key to clean product.

Above left: There are numerous commercial cleaning products for mold prevention and treatment.

Step 2: Build a vestibule

If possible, create a vestibule (a small area outside of the grow room) where you keep a clean jumpsuit or set of clothes, shoes, gloves, and sunglasses to change into before entering. There is no need for special clothing, like a Hazmat jumpsuit, but the clothes you wear in the grow room should be clean and pest free. This will prevent any spores or insect pests that attach themselves to your everyday clothes and shoes from entering the grow room. Spider mites are often carried in on shoes, but almost any insect can piggyback this way. Changing before entering the grow room will also create a habit of protecting your skin and eyes.

If you choose to use a "clean" suit, then reserve it just for wearing inside the vestibule.

GROW ROOM

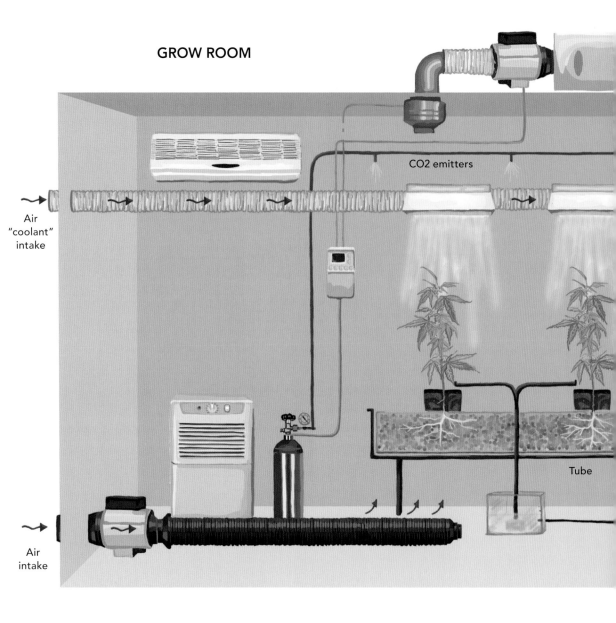

Air "coolant" intake

CO2 emitters

Air intake

Tube

In the above picture you can see the intake (air conditioner) and exhaust (fan on wall at right side of diagram).

Step 3: Add air conditioning

There should only be two entry points in any grow room: the entry/exit door and a window to hold an air conditioner. If there is no window, consider a split through-the-wall system or a standalone air conditioner. Standalone units will require an exhaust port to the outside to get rid of the heated, moisture-laden air produced by the unit. You will need a lot of cooling power—for example, a 12000-BTU air conditioner for a 10×12-foot room.

The size of the air conditioner may seem like overkill for a room that size, especially since a 10×12-foot bedroom requires a unit about half that size. But

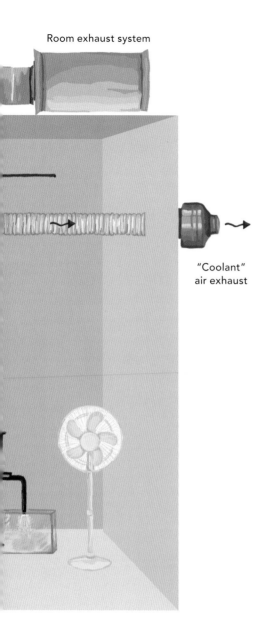

Room exhaust system

"Coolant" air exhaust

outer, or grow, room provides the cool air that is circulated through the growing chambers. To start, aim for a growing room temperature of 75°F and 50 percent humidity. You will probably need to make adjustments once your growing chambers are up and running. You will need to place a thermometer and hygrometer (to measure relative humidity) in every growing chamber and in the grow room. If your particular AC unit does not have a humidity control feature, use a room humidifier equipped with a controller and hygrometer.

Other Options

In a perfect world, everyone would be able to install the equipment that controls the cooling and humidity in their grow room. But if an AC unit is out of the question, you will at the very least need to bring fresh air into the room as well as remove hot, humid air. Remember, the air in the grow room will be used to control the environment in the growing chambers. Install a wall-mounted exhaust and intake fan on a wall. Follow the manufacturer's directions for installation, but usually installation involves using a template supplied by the manufacturer to trace the outline of the fan on a wall, cutting through the wall, and installing a mounting flange on wall studs. Choose fans that can move about twice the volume of air in the room per minute.

the environment in the grow room is going to temper the extreme temperatures of the growing chambers. For example, if your growing chambers become too hot, you may have to cool the outer room by as much as 15°F below the growing chamber temperature. As you will see in the following projects, the

To get your garden started and keep it running, you will need an area for germination, asexual reproduction, and stasis.

CO$_2$ ENHANCEMENT SYSTEMS

Plants need carbon dioxide (CO$_2$) to thrive. (See "CO$_2$ and Circulation," page 49) The two commonly used CO$_2$ enhancement systems are quick-release and burner systems.

Quick-release systems are simply bottled CO$_2$ with electric regulators attached. They can be run constantly or on a schedule by connecting the regulator on the bottle to a timer. The CO$_2$ flows from the tank through the regulator as the solenoid valve opens, through a dispensing line and into the growing environment. These systems require little electricity and have a lower initial cost than burner units. But bottled CO$_2$ is more expensive than liquid propane or natural gas, which powers the burner units, so quick-release costs more to operate in the long run. Quick-release systems create no heat and can be placed inside or outside of the growing environment. You can find complete quick-release systems that include a timer and gauges for measuring flow and amount of CO$_2$ remaining, and an electric solenoid valve regulator. CO$_2$ bottles are usually sold in 20- or 50-pound sizes.

Burner systems use liquid propane or natural gas to produce CO$_2$. The gas is fed from a bottle to a series of burners ignited by an electric spark. **Note: Do not use burners with older pilot light-style igniters or those that don't have safety cutoff switches.** Most burners are meant to be placed directly in the environment and introduce CO$_2$ through slots on the sides of the burners. Having a burner in the growing environment will raise the temperature. There are manufacturers who make burners with 6-inch or 8-inch ports on them to deliver CO$_2$ to your environment while keeping the burner outside, but the popularity of air- and water-cooled burners have made them harder to find. For safety reasons, place liquid propane or natural gas tanks *outside* of your environment; the hose supplied with most units is 12 feet long, so this shouldn't be a problem.

Burners that use heat exchangers still have slots to release CO$_2$, but they are located low on the unit, near the burners. The upper portion of the unit is enclosed so heat can be drawn up through the exchanger through a fan and out through ducting. Some people even use the exhaust from these systems to heat their homes because the exhaust is free of CO$_2$ after it passes through the heat exchanger.

Water-cooled burners use cold water and a manifold to soak up radiant heat and carry it away. They are smaller than conventional burners and have one slot located on the front of the unit to release CO$_2$. These are placed directly into the growing environment and have nozzles on the bottom for liquid propane or natural gas hookups, as well as a water-in and water-out nozzle. They can be connected directly to household water lines, or run on a closed-loop system like the icebox with a pump, reservoir, and chiller described in "Water-Cooled Circulation with Lighting System" on page 118.

Whatever method you choose, *always* follow manufacturer's instructions, place tanks outside the growing environment, and have automatic fire extinguishers on hand. Models with electric ignition and anti-tip sensors and automatic shutoffs are very safe and efficient, and will save operating costs in the long run.

Note: Some people get a queasy feeling when high CO_2 levels (1500 PPM+) are present. Not everyone reacts this way, but if you have respiratory issues such as asthma or are prone to fainting, wear a respiration mask or a simple painter's mask when you enter the growing environment to work with your plants. You can also manually turn CO_2 off and pump only non-enriched air into the environment for 10 minutes or so to raise oxygen levels to a more comfortable ratio before entering.

HOW TO BUILD A REPRODUCTION ENVIRONMENT

This small growing environment or closet is the most basic system that you can build. You can purchase kits and assemble them according to the supplied instructions, or slightly modify them. These small closets can be modified for multiple uses, but they'll start first as a place to grow clones.

Space in these growing environments is usually tight, so it is best to keep as much equipment outside of the closet as possible. You will not only save space, you will keep heat-generating equipment, such as light ballasts, outside of the growing area. You will also have to deal with many power cords. Use power strips to help keep everything organized.

Using a Purchased Tent

You can buy factory-made tents that are specifically designed for growing. They come lined with reflective material to get the most out of your lights, as well as ports for ventilation and zippered entryways for access. These are great products. They are sturdy enough to support hanging lights and fans, and they're easy to put together and take down. Moreover, the floors are designed to contain spills, and they are easy to clean. You can find them for under $200; they are worth the investment for the more novice grower.

MATERIALS

- 2×2-foot factory-made growing tent; most tents have exhaust and cord ports already in place, and some feature drawstrings on the ports to make connecting ducts and fans easier
- Air-cooled light fixture with reflector to accommodate 400-watt HPS bulb
- 400-watt HPS bulb
- Ballast
- Light hanging system, available where hydroponic equipment is sold, or chains or zip ties to hang the light
- For exhaust: blower fan rated at 200+ CFM (cubic feet per minute)
- 4-inch insulated flex duct
- For intake air: 6-inch inline duct booster fan rated at 160 CFM

- 2 6-inch to 4-inch reducers (if needed)
- Duct tape and hose clamps (optional)
- A single-bucket drip system for a mother and a 50-site propagation tray for germination or clones
- Automatic fire extinguisher
- Hand tools: long, sharp knife; wire cutters; utility knife; screwdriver; pliers

BUILD THE SYSTEM

1. Set up your tent according to the supplied instructions. In most cases, this means assembling a frame made of metal tubing that snaps into plastic connectors. The tent material has a reflective surface that faces inside the chamber. The tent is stretched over the frame. Zippers provide access to the interior.
2. Assemble the light fixture and reflector. There will be instructions, but usually the reflector screws to the top of the fixture. Screw in the bulb, and place the heat-resistant glass plate over the opening in the reflector, securing it in place.
3. Hang the lamp from the tent's ceiling supports using a manufactured hanging system, chains, or zip ties. If you are devising your own hanging system, loop the chains over the crossbars in the ceiling of the tent. Or use S-hooks placed on the crossbars. Attach the chains to holes in the top of the reflector. For clones, place the light about 30 inches above the tray.
4. Measure a length of duct that can run from the port of the reflector up through the ventilation port in the top of the tent and down to the floor of the grow room (outside the tent). Cut the duct by using the long knife to cut through the insulation; use wire cutters to cut the wire.
5. Connect the duct to the port on the reflector using duct tape. Pull back the insulation to expose the duct; make sure the duct covers the reflector port. Secure with duct tape.
6. Run the ducting up through the ventilation port in the ceiling of the tent. You can run the duct out of the tent and down to the floor of the grow room, outside the growing chamber. (Consult the manufacturer's instructions.) Connect the fan to the duct using duct tape or hose clamps.
7. To provide intake air, connect the duct booster fan to the port located near the bottom of the tent. Many of the prefab ports on smaller tents are 4 inches in diameter. If that is the case with your tent, use one of the duct reducers to connect the fan to the port. Install the other reducer on the outlet side of the fan, securing the connections with duct tape. Combining the booster fan and the reducers creates an inexpensive inline fan.
8. Run all power cords through the port provided. The cord for the light fixture will plug into the ballast. Place the light's ballast outside the tent near where the power cords will be plugged in.
9. Place the propagation tray and the mothers in the tent.

USE THE SYSTEM

Plug in the power cords to start the fans and lighting system.

Timers aren't necessary for your lamp. These small chambers run very effectively at 24 hours of constant light for peak production. If the mother plant is growing too fast, or if you want to slow production for any reason, use a timer to turn the lights off for 6 hours a day, simulating night. The 400-watt HPS light will work well for rooting clones at a distance of 30-plus inches, but placing it closer may be too much depending on the plants you are propagating. Keep this in mind when hanging the light. With this type of setup, at 24 hours of light a day, you can expect a healthy, reproductive mother and up to 45-plus daughter plants every 10 to 14 days.

TIP: For a slightly larger closet and double the production, a 4-foot-wide × 2-foot-deep × 7-foot-high tent/closet can be used with the same equipment. Set it up the same way, but double the mother sites and trays inside. This size tent can easily accommodate two mothers and two trays for up to 90-plus daughters every 10 to 14 days, or a staggered 45-plus every 5 to 7 days.

BUILDING YOUR OWN PRODUCTION CLOSET

Rather than purchasing a grow tent, you can covert standard-issue, ready-made wardrobes or even unpainted solid-wood furniture into a production closet. For example, you can convert a 4-foot-wide × 2-foot-deep wardrobe into a chamber that will hold 6 to 12 mothers, a flood and drain watering system, and an overhead reproduction chamber that will provide 180 daughter plants every 10 to 14 days, or 45-plus every 3 days.

MATERIALS

- 4-foot-wide × 2-foot-deep wardrobe closet with interior shelf and double doors
- Drill with 4-inch and 4½-inch hole saw attachments
- Black 6-millimeter polar plastic sheeting
- Staple gun
- 2 self-adhesive tarp zippers
- Duct tape
- Utility knife
- Air-cooled light fixture with reflector
- Ballast
- 400-watt HPS bulb
- 3 3-foot T8 dual spectrum grow lights with fixtures
- For exhaust: 1 blower fan rated about 265 CFM
- 4-inch insulated flex duct

- For intake air: 6-in. inline duct booster fan rated at 160 CFM
- 2 6-inch to 4-inch reducers (if needed)
- Screw-in hooks, chains, zip ties
- Environmental controls (thermostat, hygrometer)
- Automatic fire extinguisher
- Hand tools: long, sharp knife; wire cutters; utility knife; screwdriver; pliers

BUILD THE SYSTEM

1. Assemble the closet according to the manufacturer's instructions, up to the point where you would attach the double doors.
2. Drill a 4-inch hole into the side of the unit for the intake port. Locate the hole about 30 inches up from the floor of the closet. The hole should be on the same side of the closet as the open port on the reflector will be. This will force air in so that it circulates properly.
3. Drill a 4½-inch hole in the overhead shelf on the opposite side as the intake (intake right, exhaust left) and a 4-inch hole directly above the shelf in the ceiling of the unit for the exhaust.
4. Cut a piece of opaque plastic sheeting 4 feet, 8 inches × 7 feet, 6 inches. Staple the sheeting to the front of the unit so that 4 inches overhang the top, bottom, and sides.
5. Secure the overhang with staples and duct tape on the top and sides. Cut slits in the sheeting for the door hinges.
6. Attach the tarp zippers about 4 inches in from the hinge slits on each side of the opening, and about 4 inches from the top. The zipper is flanked by adhesive strips. Remove the covering and press the adhesive into place. The zippers should unzip from the bottom to the top.
7. Once attached, open up the zippers and use a utility knife to cut the sheeting beneath the zipper. Now you can zip open your closet, roll up the flap, and place the roll on the roof of the closet while you are tending to your plants.
8. Attach the T8 fixture to the ceiling of the unit. If you can't screw the fixture directly to the ceiling, use screw-in hooks and hang the fixture from the hooks using chains or zip ties.
9. If it's not already assembled, assemble the reflector on the HPS light fixture. Install the bulb and the heat-resistant glass plate.
10. Attach the assembly to the underside of the shelf in the unit, using screw-in hooks, chains, or zip ties as described above.
11. Using duct tape, attach the duct to the exhaust port on the light fixture. (See Steps 4 and 5 of "Using a Purchased Tent." on page 103) Run the duct through the hole in the shelf and out the hole in the ceiling of the unit.
12. Place the exhaust fan on the roof of the closet. Use duct tape to connect the duct to the blower.
13. Install the intake fan as described in "Using a Purchased Tent" on page 103.

As an alternative to free up some room inside the closet, place the intake fan outside the unit and connect it to the hole you drilled with ducting. Screw a duct flange around the hole on the exterior wall and connect the duct using duct tape or hose clamps.

14. Drill holes to run power cords outside of the closet. The cord from the light fixture will plug into the ballast, which should be placed outside of the closet.

15. Hang the fire extinguisher above the unit.

16. Install the environmental controls inside the chamber on the shelf or screw them to a sidewall if possible. Place them where they will be out of your way while working but easy to read. Place the watering system and plants in the chamber.

17. Install the closet doors.

USE THE SYSTEM

Plug in the cords to start the fans and the lighting system.

The T8 dual-spectrum grow lights cost about $10 each. They give off a purplish light that is better for the clones than the blue 6500K T5, and the T8s are a bargain compared to the 3-foot T5 setups.

Propagation chambers require as much as twice the maintenance of veg or flower chambers. Be sure to monitor the environmental conditions in the chambers daily. Check on the condition of both the mothers and the clones. Develop a routine of checking water levels and spraying clone trays with water to maximize take rates.

TIP: An alternate to a DIY wardrobe closet is a framed structure constructed with 1 × 2 lumber. Draw out the dimensions you want for the closet, and lay out the walls on the floor. Attach what would be the wall studs to a top and bottom plate with butt joints, driving 2-inch screws through the joints. Drive screws through the corners to join walls and build the closet. Clad the walls in black plastic sheeting that is at least 6 millimeters thick. Or you can cover the back and sidewalls with ¼-inch plywood. Construct a roll-up front out of plastic sheeting and tarp zippers as described in "Building Your Own Production Closet," page 105.

CIRCULATION SYSTEMS

The circulation system in your growing chambers helps control the environmental factors that affect the plants. The ideal conditions are:

- Relative humidity: between 40 and 60 percent
- Temperature: between 68°F to 75°F
- Carbon dioxide saturation: 300 to 400 PPM of CO_2

There are four different systems for arranging lighting and fans to maintain the ideal conditions:

- Simple circulation system
- Circulation with air-cooled lighting system
- Circulation with closed-loop lighting system
- Circulation with water-cooled lighting system

The projects that follow show how to set up these circulation systems. They are based on chambers that measure 8×4×7 feet. These are larger than the chambers covered earlier, and they are suited for the vegetative and flowering stages of your plants. Be sure to read Chapter 8: Production Techniques, page 153 to help plan the chambers needed for your garden.

SIMPLE CIRCULATION SYSTEM

Simple circulation is the oldest and most common circulation system. It consists of a light hung inside a reflector. An intake fan moves two to three times as much air per hour as the room contains. In this system, the air circulation creates a positively charged environment (a room with more air flowing *in* than out). A positively charged environment gives plants time to make full use of the CO_2 available.

MATERIALS

- 8×4×7-foot grow room tent, or a custom-built structure of approximately the same size
- Light fixture with reflector
- 1000-watt HPS bulb
- Ballast
- Hanging accessories available where hydroponic equipment is sold, or chains or zip ties for hanging the light fixture
- 2 inline fans that can move double the tent's volume per minute; in this case, at least 448 CFM
- Insulated flex duct (sized to fit the tent's ports and fans)
- Duct reducers (if necessary to adapt ducts to equipment)
- Duct tape
- Thermostat and fan speed controller
- CO_2 monitor
- Large oscillating fan
- Hand tools: long, sharp knife; wire cutters; utility knife; screwdriver; pliers
- Plant watering system (see Chapter 5, page 63)

BUILD THE SYSTEM

1. Set up the grow room tent. Follow the manufacturer's directions, but setup usually consists of assembling a metal frame using connectors. Stretch the tent material over the frame.
2. Attach the hanging system or the chains to the holes on the top of the

reflector. (See "Light" in Chapter 3, page 44, for recommendations on positioning lights above plants.) Hang the light fixture from the metal crossbars on the tent's ceiling. (See "Using a Purchased Tent," page 103.) Install the bulb.

3. Run the cord for the light fixture through the cord port so that is outside of the tent. This cord plugs into the ballast, which can be placed on the floor or on a table outside of the tent. Some ballasts come with a hanging flange so that they can be hung vertically.

4. Install the exhaust fan in one of the upper ports. Many tents contain sleeves or cuffs where you can insert the fan. Use duct tape to seal the connection. To support the fan in a horizontal position, loop or attach zip ties or chains over the crossbar and through the mounting bracket on the fan.

5. Install an intake fan in one of the lower ports on the side of tent opposite the exhaust fan. First run the flex duct from the port to outside of the tent. Attach the ducting to the port flap using duct tape. Some tents have drawstrings to attach the ducts. Set up the fan outside of the tent and attach the ducting to it.

6. Place the oscillating fan inside the chamber and run its cord outside of the chamber. Position the fan so as it swings from side to side it circulates the air around the plants.

7. Install a combination thermostat and fan speed controller by plugging the exhaust fan into the controller. Place the CO_2 monitor.

USE THE SYSTEM

Place your watering system in position. Plug in the cords to start the fans and the lighting system.

The exhaust fan pulls hot air out at a rate controlled by the thermostat and a fan speed controller. Set the controller so that as the heat in the room rises above 75°F, the exhaust fan will speed up. If the temperature dips below 68°F, the exhaust fan will slow to idle setting to allow the lamp to heat the room enough to keep it within range. If the temperature moving out of the desired range is a consistent problem, you can control the intake fan speed by plugging it into the controller. Slowing down the intake fan will change the room from positively charged to neutral, but CO_2 should stay close to desired levels. If you are forced to choose between a low temperature and a little less CO_2, go with less CO_2. It is important to keep respiration at proper levels, and respiration slows more when temperatures are too low or too high than it slows with lower CO_2 intake.

This system is relatively inexpensive and will provide a good growing environment as long as the grow room where the chamber sits is kept cool enough and has sufficient airflow. The main disadvantage of this system is that the hot high-intensity discharge light (HID) must be kept at a greater distance from your plants than with other types of systems. Fewer lumens reach the plants the farther away the light source is, wasting electricity.

CIRCULATION WITH AIR-COOLED LIGHTING SYSTEM

This system was developed to increase yield and efficiency. Lighting companies started building enclosed reflectors so that growers could cool the lamp itself, allowing greater control of air temperature and light by reducing radiant heat from the lamp. A cooler lamp can be hung closer to the plants, greatly increasing lumens at the growth site.

An air-cooled reflector is basically a box or enclosed space with a reflector over the lamp to direct and reflect light, a tempered plate glass panel to allow light to pass through but keep heat in. A separate fan pulls the heat from the fixture and out of the chamber.

MATERIALS

8×4×7-foot grow room tent, or a custom-built structure of approximately the same size. Plant watering systems (see Chapter 5, page 63)

A Air-cooled light fixture

B 1000-watt HPS bulb

C Ballast

D Hanging accessories available where hydroponic equipment is sold, or chains or zip ties for hanging the light fixture

E Flexible duct sized to fit the exhaust port of the light

F 2 inline fans that can move double the tent's volume per minute; in this case, at least 448 CFM

G Duct reducers (if the fan is larger than the tent's ports, usually 8- to 6-inch reducers)

H Duct tape or zip ties

I Oscillating fan

J Thermostat with fan controller

Some equipment you'll need for your grow room can be obtained from any hardware store. Most of the circulation system supplies can be found at a hydroponic speciality store.

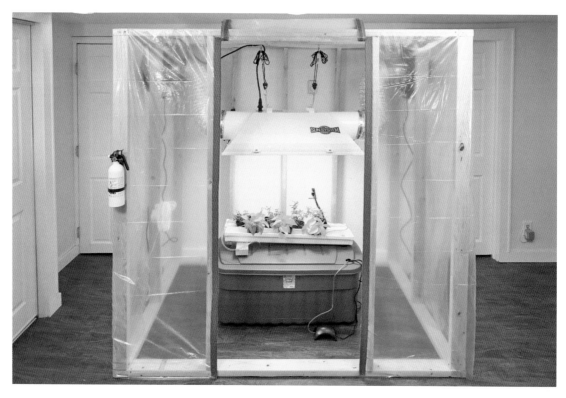

BUILD THE SYSTEM

Steps 1 through 3 are the same as described under Simple Circulation, page 108.

Above: Use clear polar plastic so you can easily view your setup.

1. Set up the grow room tent. You can build your own rooms with wood studs and sheet plastic. Or, you can buy a tent kit. If you buy a kit, follow the manufacturer's directions, but setup usually consists of assembling a metal frame using connectors. Stretch the tent material over the frame. If you are making a DIY room, wait to install the "walls" until everything else is set up.

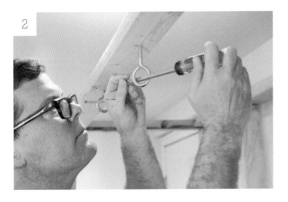

2. Install a hanging system. Attach the hanging system or the chains to the holes on the top of the reflector.

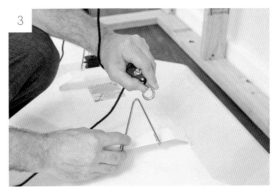

3. Hang the light fixture.

4. Adjust the light height (see "Lights" in Chapter 3, page 44)

5. Install the bulb, taking care not to handle the glass portion.

6. Run the cord for from the light fixture through the cord port so that is outside of the tent.

7. This cord plugs into the ballast, which can be placed on the floor or on a table outside of the tent. Some ballasts come with a hanging flange so that they can be hung vertically.

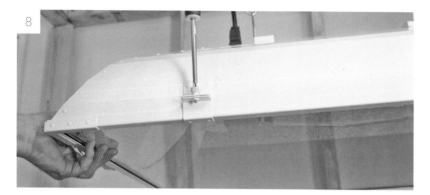

8. Install the glass panel on the reflector to enclose the bulb. Usually, it simply slides into place.

9. Install an exhaust fan in an upper port of the tent. (See Step 4 "Simple Circulation System," page 108.)

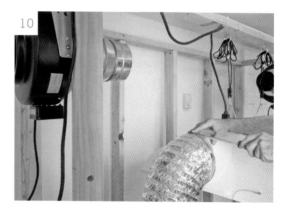

10. The fan should be lined up with the exhaust port of the lamp reflector. If you are attaching an 8-inch fan, use duct reducers to fit it into the port if necessary.

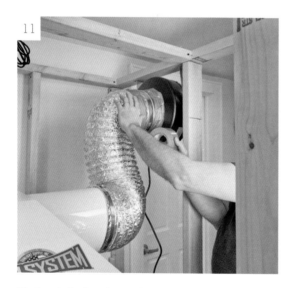

11. Attach the flex duct to the reflector exhaust port and to the fan using duct tape. Avoid making sharp turns with the duct.

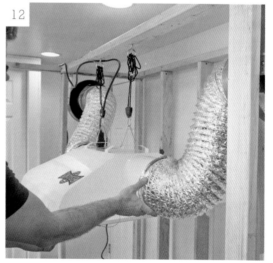

12. Install the intake fan in a lower port opposite the exhaust fan location. If necessary, use the duct reducers to fit the fan into the port. Or place the fan outside of the tent and connect it to the port by ducting.

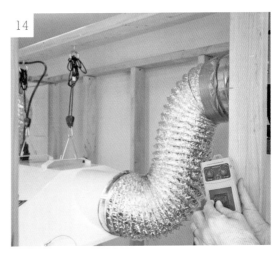

13. Place the oscillating fan inside the chamber, and run its cord outside of the chamber. Position the fan so that it circulates the air around the plants.

14. Place the environmental controls in the tent. To keep them out of the way, use Velcro to attach them to the tent's walls. Plug the exhaust fan into the fan controller.

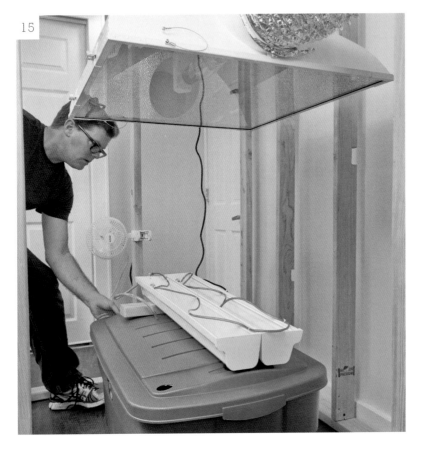

15. Position the watering system and any other system you'll use, including CO_2 enhancement systems. Install the sheet plastic walls if you have not done so already.

USE THE SYSTEM

Place your watering system in position. Plug in the cords to start the fans and the lighting system.

Generally, these reflectors do not have the coverage area of the parabolic or cone reflectors, but you can place them closer to the plants. (See "Light" in Chapter 3, page 44.) Advancements in reflective materials and light angling techniques are constantly being tested and refined to bridge this gap. The Magnum XXXL 8 is a good example. It is the equivalent of a cone in coverage area and provides a higher quality of light with its wide construction, obtuse angles, and reflective material. It also comes with 8-inch duct fittings or posts instead of the standard 6-inch, so it fits nicely with an 8-inch inline fan.

Calibrating Timers for Cooling and CO_2

If using a CO_2 enhancement system, be sure the system operates while the fans in the closet are off. Otherwise, the CO_2 will be expelled with the rest of the air, and the plants will not get time to use it. To set up a schedule, you will need timers for both the CO_2 system and the fans. Program the timers by turning the light on and setting the fans to cool the environment to the lowest ideal temperature (68°F). At that temperature, turn the fans off, and time how long it takes to reach the high end of the desired temperature range (75°F). This is the time you can leave the intake and exhaust fans off before the temperature will rise above the desired level—and thus how long you can pump CO_2 in. When the temperature again reaches the high, turn the fans back on and time how long they take to cool the environment. This gives you the time you will need to have your fans on and CO_2 off to keep the environment cool.

For example, if an environment takes 30 minutes to increase from 68°F to 75°F with the light on and fans off, and 15 minutes to cool from 75 to 68°F with the fans on, you would set the timer on the CO_2 for 30 minutes on and 15 minutes off. The fans would run on the opposite schedule; 15 minutes on, 30 minutes off.

Remember that circulation is always affected by the temperature of intake air, so if your intake comes directly from outside, and the air is hot, the indoor growing environment will be slower to cool. With cold temperatures outside, the indoor environment will cool quicker, so adjust the fans and CO_2 accordingly.

An inexpensive in-line timer controls the environmental systems in the grow room.

Some professionals and enthusiasts consider these CO_2-enriched circulating systems to be wasteful because CO_2 cannot be completely consumed by the plants and is flushed out at intervals by the fans. But in reality, CO_2 is slightly heavier than oxygen, so as long as a circulation fan keeps it from concentrating on the floor, it never needs to be flushed out. This is where the closed-loop system, following, shines—it conserves CO_2 concentration.

TIP: An alternative to a stationary hanging system is a motorized rail that travels back and forth at 6 to 10 rpm. This allows you to get double the coverage and maximum lumens by physically moving your light back and forth over the growing zone. The light rail 3.5 (about $250) is a relatively inexpensive way to double a 1000-watt HID's coverage and greatly increase the amount of lumens in your growing zone. It also eliminates hot spots and allows you to get the light slightly closer to plants because the light is moving back and forth and won't cook precious new vertical growth. If using a pre-fab growing tent, check to make sure the ceiling supports can hold and accommodate the light mover. If you are using a room with a solid ceiling, attach the track to the ceiling joists using screws. Place the motor in the track and attach the lights to the motor.

CIRCULATION WITH CLOSED-LOOP LIGHTING SYSTEM

"Closed loop" refers to the way the lamp is cooled. To minimize CO_2 waste and achieve greater control over the temperature of the growing environment, both the intake and exhaust fans are mounted to the ports on the air-cooled hood. They are pointed in the same direction and ducted directly in and out of the lamp hood. Fresh air is brought only into and directly out through the lamp housing, so CO_2 feeds the plants through enrichment (either quick-release or a burner). A separate exhaust fan can be used as a fail-safe method in case temperatures climb too high.

MATERIALS

- 8×4×7-foot grow room tent, or a custom-built structure of approximately the same size
- Air-cooled light fixture
- 1000-watt HPS bulb
- Ballast
- Hanging accessories available where hydroponic equipment is sold, or chains or zip ties for hanging the light fixture
- Insulated flexible duct sized to fit the ports of the light
- 2 inline fans that can move about 450 CFM; these can be 6- or 8-inch fans
- Duct reducers (if the fan is larger than the fixture's ports, usually 8- to 6-inch reducers)
- Duct tape or zip ties
- 18-inch oscillating fan
- Thermostat with fan controller
- CO_2 enrichment system (optional)
- Hand tools: long, sharp knife; wire cutters; utility knife; screwdriver; pliers
- Watering system that uses a reservoir (see "Reservoir Systems," page 83)

BUILD THE SYSTEM

1–3. Follow Steps 1 through 3 as noted in Simple Circulation, page 108.

4. Mount the fans directly to the intake and exhaust ports of the fan. The fans should point in the same direction. Secure with duct tape. Use duct reducers if the fans and port openings do not match.

5. Run ducting from the fans to the ports on the sides of the enclosure. Secure the ducting in the port sleeves using duct tape.

Optional: If mounting two fans directly to your fixture makes it too heavy, you can mount the fans to the ports on the sidewalls of the enclosure, or install one on the fixture and one on a sidewall. (See Step 3 in "Using a Purchased Tent," page 103.) The key is to direct air in and out of the light fixture so that it stays separate from the growing environment.

CLOSED LOOP COOLED SYSTEM

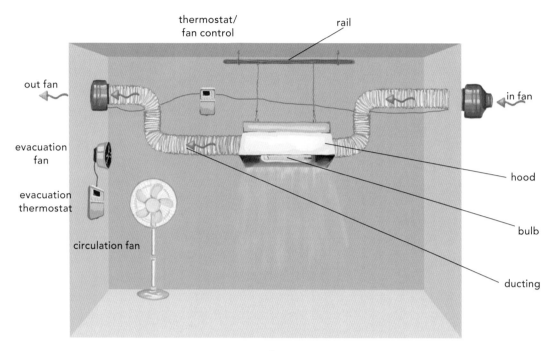

4x8x7-foot tent

6. Plug the fans into a controller with a sensor that allows for temperature control by controlling fan speed. Mount the controller where it will be easily accessible, using Velcro fasteners or zip ties.

7. Place the oscillating fan in the tent so that it circulates the air around the plants.

8. If using, connect the CO_2 enhancement system. For a quick-release system, attach the regulator to the bottle by tightening the nut on the regulator. Set the release pressure by opening the valve and watching the pressure gauge. Plug the system into a controller. Always read and follow the manufacturer's directions.

9. Connect the watering system, but place the reservoir outside of the growing chamber.

CIRCULATION WITH WATER-COOLED LIGHTING SYSTEM

In a closed-loop system, you'll enrich the growing environment with CO_2 via your preferred method. Because the plants will get oxygen via their roots through the air pump enriching the nutrient solution, make sure that you locate the air pump in the nutrient solution outside of the growing environment, where oxygen levels are normal.

The exhaust fan pulls hot air out at a rate controlled by the thermostat and a fan speed controller. Set the controller so that as the heat in the room rises above 75°F, the exhaust fan will speed up. If the temperature dips below 68°F, the exhaust fan will slow to idle setting to allow the lamp to heat the room enough to keep it within range. If the temperature moving out of the desired range is a consistent problem, you can control the intake fan speed by plugging it into the controller.

For some professionals and enthusiasts, the variables in temperature and humidity caused by using air from outside the growing area are undesirable. Water-cooled lights have become the preferred circulation system for maximum control of environmental factors. Water-cooling has been around since the 1970s, but early equipment was poorly designed and had to be plumbed into existing water lines. The development of "chillers" and "iceboxes" over the last few years has changed all that. Chillers are electric water-cooling boxes that use internal heat exchangers and compressors to cool water. They allow you to use a reservoir of water and a pump to deliver cold water to water-cooled lamp systems. For every 1000 watts of lamp, use ¼ horsepower in chiller size (so four 1000-watt HPS lights would require 1 horsepower of chiller size).

MATERIALS

- Reservoir (see page 83)
- Chiller
- Water pump (sized per chiller manufacturer specifications)
- Irrigation tubing
- Hose clamps if necessary
- 1000-watt HID lamp
- Ballast
- Water-cooled light fixture
- Timers
- Environmental controls: thermostat, hydrometer
- CO_2 enrichment system
- Hand tools: long, sharp knife; wire cutters; utility knife; screwdriver; pliers
- Plant watering system (see Chapter 5, page 63)

WATER AIRFLOW FOR WATER-COOLED LIGHTING SYSTEM

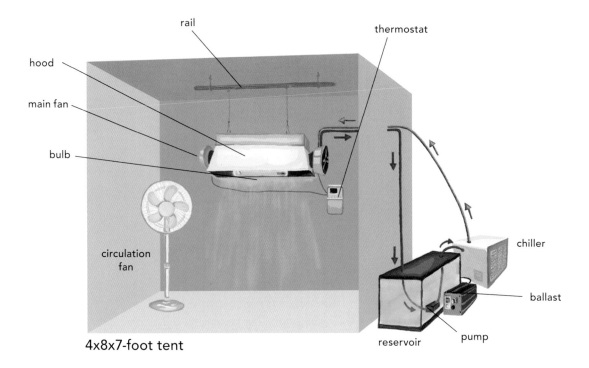

4x8x7-foot tent

BUILD THE SYSTEM

1–3. Follow Steps 1 through 3 as described in Simple Circulation, page 108.

4. Outside of the chamber, construct a reservoir and fill it with at least 30 gallons of clean water. The manufacturer will give the specifications of GPM (gallons per minute) the chiller needs to operate properly. For example, an enclosure equipped with one 1000-watt HID lamp and a ¼-horsepower chiller would require about a 1056-GPM pump.

5. Connect the reservoir's pump to the chiller inlet nozzle with ¾-inch poly-tube. These are usually barbed fittings, so just push them into place. Use hose clamps if your unit does not have barbed fittings. (Locate the reservoir and the chiller outside of the growing environment because both can elevate humidity and heat levels.)

6. Run polytube to your water-cooled lighting system from the chiller's outlet nozzle. Water-cooled light fixtures have nipples to make the connection. Make the connection using hose clamps.

7. Use polytube to connect the outgoing nozzle on your water-cooled lighting system to the reservoir.

8. Plug everything in. Program the chiller to the desired temperature range (follow the manufacturer's instructions). Test the water-cooling system without any plants or lights in place to make sure everything is operational and there are no leaks. You'll know it is working if the temperature, humidity, and CO_2 levels remain in the ideal range.

9. Place oscillating fan and controls in the chamber. Position the fan so that it circulates the air around the plants.
10. For a quick-release system CO_2 enhancement system, attach the regulator to the bottle by tightening the nut on the regulator. Set the release pressure by opening the valve and watching the pressure gauge. Plug the system into a controller. Always read and follow the manufacturer's directions.
11. Install the plant watering system.

USE THE SYSTEM

If your lights are on a timer, synchronize another timer to shut off the pump and chiller at the same time to conserve energy. A ¼-horsepower chiller pulls 480 watts of electricity at 4 amps.

ICEBOXES

An "icebox" is a heat exchanger in a plastic housing designed to cool air with water, similar to the way a radiator in a car works (although in a car, air is cooling water). It is similar to the water-cooled system except you use it with an air-cooled light. Cold water runs through the manifold of the heat exchanger. As the fan draws warm air into the icebox, the water absorbs the air's heat, carrying it away and cycling back to the reservoir. The cooled air is drawn through the reflector housing to cool the lamp.

MATERIALS

- Reservoir and chiller system
- Icebox heat exchanger (sized to match the port on the light reflector)
- Air-cooled lighting fixture
- 100-watt lamp
- Ballast
- Hanging system
- Polytubing (sized to fit the icebox and chiller connections)
- Hose clamps
- Inline fan that can move about 450 CFM
- Insulated flex duct
- Duct reducers (if the fan is larger than the fixture's ports, usually 8- to 6-inch reducers)
- Duct tape and zip ties
- 18-inch oscillating fan
- Thermostat with fan controller
- CO_2 enrichment system
- Hand tools: long, sharp knife; wire cutters; utility knife; screwdriver; pliers
- Plant watering system (see Chapter 5, page 63)

BUILD THE SYSTEM

1.–3. Follow Steps 1 through 3 as described in Simple Circulation, page 108.

4. Set up the same reservoir and chiller system as described above (or on page 119).

5. Connect the icebox to the intake port of the reflector. Use duct tape and hose clamps to make the connection.

6. Connect the inline fan to the other end of the hood using duct tape and hose clamps or zip ties. This pushes the air in the environment past the lamp and through the heat exchanger so that it is cooled as it reenters the growing environment.

7. Plug the inline fan into a thermostat with fan control. This will give control over growing environment temperature, along with the option to maintain an enclosed environment that conserves CO_2.

8. Use the polytube to connect the intake nipple on the icebox to the nipple on the chiller. Secure the connection with hose clamps.

9. Connect the outflow nipple on the icebox with the reservoir with the polytube.

10. Position the oscillating fan so that it circulates the air around the plants.

11. For a quick-release system CO_2 enhancement system, attach the regulator to the bottle by tightening the nut on the regulator. Set the release pressure by opening the valve and watching the pressure gauge. Plug the system into a controller. Always read and follow the manufacturer's directions.

12. Install the plant watering system.

CHAPTER 7

Creating a Nutrient Solution

I n order to correctly mix a nutrient solution, you need to be able to read fertilizer labels. Whether you're using one packaged fertilizer or mixing several different components together, understanding these calculations is an absolute must. Here's how to do it:

Ready to Use

FERTIFEED
All Purpose Plant Food

12-4-8

FertiFeed Ready To Use All-Purpose Plant Food
Net Weight 4lb. 12oz. (2.15kg)

GUARANTEED ANALYSIS
Total Nitrogen (N)..12%
    12.0% Urea Nitrogen
Available Phosphate (P_2O_5).....................................4%
Soluable Potash (K2O)..8%
Manganese (Mn)..0.05%
    0.05% Chelated Manganese (Mn)
Zinc (Zn) 0.05%
    0.05% Chelated Zinc (Zn)
Inert Ingredients..76%

Information regarding the contents and levels of metals in this product is available on the Internet at http://www.regulatory-info-sc.com.

KEEP OUT OF REACH OF CHILDREN

Understanding labels allows you to cut costs and avoid mistakes.

Opposite: Use precise measurements and work carefully when blending your nutrient solution.

MACRONUTRIENTS

Nitrogen Deficiency

Nitrogen Abundance

Phosphorus Deficiency

Potassium Deficiency

Sulfur Deficiency

Calcium Deficiency

THE PRIMARY MACRONUTRIENTS

The primary macronutrients are the main three nutrients used by plants in the largest quantities.

Nitrogen

Discovered in Scotland by Daniel Rutherford in 1772 and named by J. A. Chaptal in 1790, nitrogen is an odorless, colorless, tasteless gaseous chemical element that forms nearly four-fifths of the world's atmosphere. Nitrogen is a component of all proteins and nucleic acids, so it is present in every living cell. Nitrogen is an essential building block that plays an essential role in chlorophyll synthesis, so it's necessary for photosynthesis. This is why a nitrogen-deficient plant goes from green, an indicator of prevalent healthy chlorophyll, to yellow. Nitrogen-deficient plants are literally running out of the element used to make the green chlorophyll molecules. Without nitrogen and chlorophyll, a plant can't use sunlight as an energy source to carry on essential functions, including sugar production and nutrient uptake.

PLANT USE OF NITROGEN

- The principle element used in the vegetative growth phase
- Part of all living cells
- A necessary part of amino acids, the building blocks of proteins and enzymes
- A necessary part of the metabolic processes that make and transfer energy
- A necessary part of chlorophyll, the green part of plants responsible for photosynthesis
- Used to repair plants that yellow during heavy blooming due to lack of its presence, and can even be used to slow blooming, or return a blooming plant to the vegetative growth phase

SYMPTOMS OF NITROGEN DEFICIENCY

A nitrogen deficiency causes chlorosis, the yellowing of green foliage. This yellowing will have a background look, like the green leaf was painted on a yellow canvas, getting more severe and more yellow as the deficiency persists. Plant growth will begin to look stunted and slow down to the point of cell death.

HOW TO CORRECT A NITROGEN DEFICIENCY

To treat a deficiency in a nutrient solution, diagnose the reason for the deficiency first. Check pH, EC, and water temperature. If these are all what they should be, you can introduce a supplemental nitrogen source of your choice, or change out your solution to a fresh one with a little bit more nitrogen in it. Take care to keep EC below 4, and go easy on the amount you put in so as not to burn plants right after they are stressed from the deficiency.

There are some great tonics on the market that contain N-P-K, micronutrients, and vitamins in combinations formulated to restore and prevent damage from deficiencies, and work well for nitrogen deficiencies.

Nitrogen deficiency slows plant growth.

SYMPTOMS OF NITROGEN OVERDOSE

Nitrogen overdose causes leaves to curl, dry, yellow, and even die at the leaf edges and tips, which then appear burnt. Leaves can also discolor in spotted patterns, become brittle to the touch, yellow at the stem, and even fall off the plant altogether.

The line is thin between maximum fertilization and tip burn.

Symptoms can be pronounced and obvious or mild and difficult to diagnose. Nitrogen overdose is a form of salt injury and can look similar to damage from high temperatures. As always, check pH, EC, water temperature, and environmental conditions and use a process of elimination to help you diagnose. The severity of symptoms will be greater the higher the overdose and the longer it continues.

Over time, spindly damaged growth, stunting, and plant death will occur. If leaves are more than 60 percent damaged by this or any other deficiency or overdose, remove them. They become hosts for disease, mold, bacteria, and pests, so your plants will be better off without them. Do *not*, however, remove more than 50 percent of the foliage from a plant at a time; this will send it into shock and create a large number of open wounds at once that can become hosts for disease, mold, bacteria, and pests.

HOW TO CORRECT A NITROGEN OVERDOSE

To correct an overdose, remove one-third of the damaged leaves, wait the lifetime of your solution (5, 7, or 10 days), and remove another one-third of the damaged leaves. Repeat until the plant has recovered and no damaged leaves remain. (Note that leaves *grow fast!*)

There are two ways to correct an overdose:

- Remove 5 to 10 gallons of solution and replace with water to dilute the solution until your next scheduled solution change.
- Immediately change the solution, recalculating the ingredients to compensate. (See the following paragraph.)

In a nitrogen overdose, this means you calculate how much you are overfeeding nitrogen and formulate your solution to have less nitrogen. The two common ways people overdose include using too much grow or bloom fertilizer and not factoring in the N-P-K analysis of every component of your solution. Follow the manufacturer's recommendations for your base grow or bloom solution and be aware of the contents of your supplements and additives, factoring in those contents when calculating your solution's total contents. Always check pH, EC, water temperature, and oxygen content after you mix the solution and before you feed.

Phosphorus

Discovered in 1669 in Germany by Hennig Brand, phosphorus is a nonmetallic chemical element. It's normally a white, wavy solid that emits a glow, but it becomes yellow when exposed to oxygen. Phosphorus in its pure form is poisonous and unites easily with oxygen, igniting at room temperature. In nature, phosphorus is not found in its pure elemental form, mostly because it is so reactive and combines with oxygen when exposed to air.

There are many different compounds that can be used to feed plants phosphorus, but the vast majority start out as phosphate rock; that is, any rock containing larger amounts of phosphorite, a combination of calcium and phosphorus. It is then broken down into an acid or base (orthophosphate PO_4^{3-}) and combined with nitrate or potassium to form soluble crystal or a salt, or simply removed from its rock form and left connected to the calcium ions. Most forms of phosphorus aren't water soluble and stay connected to some form of sediment, but in a nutrient solution you will really only be dealing with available phosphorus. These are phosphate ions that have attached to water, hydrogen, oxygen, or a nutrient in the solution to which roots can access such as calcium, magnesium, aluminum, or iron.

Phosphorus is an integral part of several chemical processes in plants. It is essential to cell division and enlargement; photosynthesis; respiration; transferring and storing energy, resisting stress; formation of oils, sugars, and starches; proper maturation; root growth; and the building of the plant's DNA.

Early in a plant's life, the majority of phosphorus will be used to create new cells and DNA for growth, but as the plant reaches maturity, phosphorus replaces nitrogen as the most important nutrient. Phosphorus remains key to plant growth and energy transfer within cells, but as flowering begins the amount of phosphorus available will directly affect the number of blooms you have, their size, the speed of their growth, and the size of the fruit and seeds.

Simply put, more phosphorus at the flowering stage means higher yields. Phosphorus levels also affect the enzyme and hormone production responsible for the change in plants from vegetative growth to flowering. Many professionals and enthusiasts now feed plants large doses of phosphorus, or specific phosphorus amounts, weeks before photoperiod change to chemically trigger flowering. This process has been proven to create higher yields in shorter time. It can even cause a rapid stop of vertical growth and force plants into the flowering before you change the photoperiod. This is called "chemical induction" or "chemically forcing" flowering. Use this technique 1 to 2 weeks before photoperiod change indoors, and it should cut your flowering time down by a week or so. Outdoors, this technique can be used up to a month before flowering would naturally occur, giving plants that wouldn't normally finish flowering or fruiting in your area due to a short season a much better chance.

These two unique properties of phosphorus, combined with nitrogen's ability to hinder flowering, are why "bloom" solutions containing more phosphorus than nitrogen are now commonly used to meet the nutritional needs of flowering plants.

The three main sources of phosphorus used in fertilizers are the organic or synthetic phosphates (organic matter, bone meal, phosphate rock, or any of the salts derived by combining phosphate with other macronutrients), chelated phosphate (two or more phosphorus chains combined with a metal ion to form a closed loop using a synthetic acid or an organic lignin), and superphosphate (monobasic calcium phosphate and gypsum made by treating bone, phosphate rock, or other sources with sulfuric acid to concentrate them).

Only feed your plants chelated phosphates when you want to bring your plants into flower; they are taken up quickly and their specific profile is the most likely to cause chemical induction at low concentrations.

PLANT USE OF PHOSPHOROUS

- The principle element used in the flowering growth stage
- Used to produce DNA
- Needed for cell division
- Necessary for cell enlargement
- Essential for photosynthesis
- Necessary for respiration
- Essential for energy storage and transfer
- Used to initiate blooming, encourage proper maturation and root growth, assist the transforming of solar energy into chemical energy, withstand stress, and even stop vertical growth

Phosphorus-deficient plant.

SYMPTOMS OF PHOSPHORUS DEFICIENCY

A phosphorus deficiency causes plants to take on a bluish or purplish color in their leaves or stems, and then leads to reduced growth caused by poor cell development, a reduction in flowering sites and flower size, and finally poor fruit production.

HOW TO CORRECT A PHOSPHORUS DEFICIENCY

Treat a phosphorus deficiency in a solution like any other. Recalculate your solution's contents and change it out, or add a supplemental phosphorus source. If the plants are in vegetative growth, be careful not to overdo it, which would trigger the plants to bloom.

SYMPTOMS OF PHOSPHORUS OVERDOSE

A phosphorus overdose can slow—or even stop—vertical growth or initiate blooming. More severe overdoses can cause chlorosis, leaf scorch, leaf curl, salt damage, and even necrosis in leaves.

HOW TO CORRECT A PHOSPHORUS OVERDOSE

There are two ways to correct an overdose:

- Remove 5 to 10 gallons of solution and replace with water to dilute the solution until your next scheduled solution change.
- Immediately change out the solution, recalculating the ingredients to compensate.

Potassium

Discovered in England in 1807 by Sir Humphrey Davy, potassium is a soft, silver-white, wax-like metallic chemical element. It is one of the alkali metals and oxidizes rapidly when exposed to air. Potassium exists in abundance in nature in the form of its salts. Potassium in fertilizers is derived from a largely diverse group of sources including natural salt forms, kelp meal, granite dust, greensand, wood ashes, natural brines, distillery water, manure, organic matter, and flue dust from blast furnaces, among many others. Synthetic fertilizers are produced by extracting potassium from one of these sources and combining it with a nitrate, sulfate, magnesium sulfate, chlorine, oxygen, hydrogen, or carbon to form a crystalline compound or salt that easily dissolves in water.

All of these forms of potassium are expressed in a fertilizer analysis as K_2O, which is called potash. Potash is the term used to describe potassium carbonate, potassium hydroxide, or any substance containing potassium that, when analyzed, comes up as K_2O in the analysis. Potassium is often described as being unavailable, slowly available, or readily available to plants. In a nutrient solution, you will be dealing with water-soluble potassium, which falls into the readily available category. Unavailable potassium is trapped in a crystalline substance that doesn't dissolve in water, and slowly available potassium is trapped between mineral layers that would become large sediment particles in a reservoir, quickly clogging a pump. Oxygen and temperatures directly affect potassium uptake, so make sure your reservoir is well oxygenated and in the tepid temperature range (70°F to 80°F).

Potassium plays important roles in early plant growth, including essential functions such as protein production, water use, breaking down carbohydrates, movement of minerals, ionic balance, and disease and insect resistance and recovery from their damage. It is essential for fruit formation and is involved in the activation of more than sixty enzymes that regulate the major plant growth reactions. It also works with phosphorus during a plant's flowering stage to promote the development of blooming sites, size of buds, and their reproductive organs. Potassium is often used in higher amounts during late flowering to improve the shelf life of fruit or when healthy seed production is desired.

PLANT USE OF POTASSIUM
- Essential for all growth stages
- Essential for protein synthesis
- Increases protein production
- Stimulates early growth
- Improves resistance to disease and insects
- Aids in recovery from damage by disease and insects
- Aids in the process of opening and closing of stomata, a plant's leaf pores
- Helps control ionic balance
- Improves the efficiency of water use
- Important in the breakdown of carbohydrates, providing energy for plants

- Important in the translocation of minerals
- Essential for the formulation of fruit
- Involved in the activation of more than sixty enzymes that regulate the rates of major plant growth reactions
- Used to promote the growth of root crops and food storage roots, to promote flowering throughout the flowering stage, to promote the development of reproductive organs, and to promote the development of fruit and seed crops

SYMPTOMS OF POTASSIUM DEFICIENCY

A potassium deficiency causes the margins of leaves to yellow and their leaf margins to brown. This can look like leaf scorch or the leaves can take on a dark, sickly appearance. Dead sections of leaves often fall off, making the leaves look tattered. Symptoms appear in older leaves first, but more severe deficiencies can affect newer leaves as well.

Potassium deficiencies can be corrected quickly.

HOW TO CORRECT A POTASSIUM DEFICIENCY

Treat a potassium deficiency in a solution like any other. Recalculate your solution's contents and change it out, or add a supplemental potassium source.

SYMPTOMS OF POTASSIUM OVERDOSE

A potassium overdose can look like leaf scorch, salt damage, or leaf curl. An overdose can cause necrosis and, in extreme cases, death.

HOW TO CORRECT A POTASSIUM OVERDOSE

There are two ways to correct an overdose:

- Remove 5 to 10 gallons of solution and replace with water to dilute the solution until your next scheduled solution change.
- Immediately change out the solution recalculating the ingredients to compensate. (See below.)

THE SECONDARY MACRONUTRIENTS

These nutrients are important in plant growth but plants use them in smaller doses than the primary macronutrients. For that reason they are not always included in standard plant fertilizers.

Calcium

Named in 1808 in England by Sir Humphrey Davy, calcium is a soft, silver-white, metallic chemical element. It's one of the alkaline earth metals. In nature it is found in limestone and marble chalk as well as in calcite or aragonite, or in bones, teeth, and shells. It is most often attached to other elements such as nitrogen, phosphorus, potassium, hydrogen, carbon, or oxygen. Calcium is included in fertilizers in combined forms including calcium nitrate, dolomitic lime, and gypsum, and it's also present in superphosphate.

PLANT USE OF CALCIUM

Calcium plays an essential role in plant development and overall plant health. Calcium facilitates the synthesis of pectin—the glue that holds cell walls together—and is therefore vital to the formation of new tissue in meristems (growing tips). Its presence directly impacts the strength of plant stems, leaves, and flowers. It aids fruit set and sets a foundation for normal transport and retention of other elements. It also promotes disease resistance. A calcium deficiency can have a devastating effect on plant growth.

Without sufficient calcium to form pectin, growth slows to a standstill and your plants will only be able to produce small, underdeveloped leaves, thin stems, and limited root systems.

SYMPTOMS OF CALCIUM DEFICIENCY

Calcium deficiencies start as dark green stunted growth in new foliage and, in severe or continued instances, can cause new growth to appear shriveled, off color, and even dead before it has a chance to develop. Calcium deficiencies can lead to death quickly and cause necrosis in stem root tips and leaf margins.

SYMPTOMS OF CALCIUM OVERDOSE

Calcium overdoses are uncommon but, like most macronutrient overdoses, appear as leaf scorch, curled tips, salt damage, chlorosis, and so forth. There are several very good tonics to add calcium, magnesium, and iron to calcium-deficient solutions. You can find these at brick and mortar hydroponics stores or online. Add them to your reservoir according to the manufacturer's instructions or recalculate them into your nutrient solution as a permanent supplement at that week in your feed chart or for the duration of your cycle. Be aware that most of these supplements contain nitrogen and raise the overall nitrogen content of the nutrient solution.

Cannabis benefits greatly from excess calcium in the solution.

Sulfur

A pale yellow, nonmetallic chemical element, sulfur can be found in crystalline or amorphous form. Sulfur exists in nature in a large number of chemical forms. It is often associated with rocks and minerals, but it can appear in freshwater springs and even rainwater.

In fertilizers, sulfur shows up in the form of gypsum or superphosphate, attached to another nutrient like magnesium sulfate or sulfate of potash, or as an impurity in low-grade fertilizers. Sulfur is used in the production of proteins and the formation of chlorophyll. It promotes the activity of enzymes and vitamins and plays a role in their development. It is used in large quantities during periods of vigorous growth and helps plants resist low temperatures. Sulfur improves root growth and seed production.

SYMPTOMS OF SULFUR DEFICIENCY

Sulfur deficiencies are uncommon because sulfur is usually present in adequate amounts in basic grow and bloom fertilizers and can be present in micronutrient formulations, supplements, and additives. Chlorosis, unhealthy root zones, and slow or thin development can be signs of a sulfur deficiency, but of all the nutrients it is usually the least likely culprit. To treat a sulfur deficiency find a product with a high concentration of sulfur, and add it to your solution a little at a time until the deficiency is corrected, or recalculate your solution to include it at intervals or for the entirety of your cycle.

The differences between many deficiencies can be slight—take care to diagnose correctly.

SYMPTOMS OF SULFUR OVERDOSE

Sulfur overdoses are also uncommon, but they appear to look much like the other macronutrient overdoses. Symptoms can be similar to leaf scorch or salt damage, or have a general stunting of growth.

THE PRIMARY MICRONUTRIENTS

Micronutrients are essential nutrients required by plants in smaller amounts than macronutrients. They are generally present in large enough quantities in soil; however, because you're feeding plants nutrient *solutions* and the plants can't get these nutrients from the soil, you will have to include them in your mix.

Overdoses of micronutrients are uncommon and can be difficult to diagnose. Symptoms can vary by species and can often look like environmental problems such as heat damage or oxygen deprivation to roots (overwatering). Knowledge of what the species of marijuana you're growing should look like, its requirements, and particular symptoms for specific deficiencies can greatly help in diagnosing micronutrient deficiencies. You need to know exactly what is in the nutrient solution so that you can diagnose or eliminate potential issues.

Diagnosing micronutrient deficiencies requires some detective work and a process of elimination because they play supporting roles in most plant functions, so they look like more common deficiencies or problems. Check environmental conditions, nutrient solution contents, and specific species nutritional needs and attempt to eliminate all other possible reasons for symptoms.

Common Micronutrient Deficiencies and Causes

Some common symptoms of micronutrient deficiencies and their culprits are:

Boron deficiencies can sometimes manifest as problems with roots, but this can easily be misdiagnosed or too subtle to diagnose.

MICRONUTRIENTS

Iron Deficiency

Molybdenum Deficiency

Zinc Deficiency

Copper Deficiency

Magnesium Deficiency

Boron Deficiency

Symptoms of New (Young) Leaves
- Dark or twisted
- Purple or blue undertones
- Metallic sheen on leaves
- Leaves turn under
- Tips may turn yellow or white

Symptoms of Older Leaves
- Older leaves may show signs of pale yellow or white.

Other Copper Deficiency Symptoms
- Buds do not ripen or grow very slowly
- Pistils (hairs) on female plants may not grow properly
- Plant may wilt or have limp leaves
- New growth has difficulty opening up

It is unlikely that there is no copper available in your water or soil, so usually a copper deficiency in cannabis is caused by a pH problem at the roots that is restricting access to nutrients.

Iron deficiencies commonly show up as chlorosis of young leaves, but because iron uptake is slowed in alkaline conditions, lowering the pH can help correct it.

Magnesium deficiencies show up as chlorosis in old leaves. Familiarize yourself with what a nitrogen deficiency looks like, and you can usually see the subtle differences between the two. Iron and magnesium play important supporting roles in chlorophyll production, so these symptoms make sense.

Molybdenum aids in nitrogen use and efficiency, so it is very difficult to differentiate from a nitrogen deficiency.

Zinc, chloride, copper, and manganese deficiencies sometimes don't show symptoms at all, and when they do they look so much like a potassium deficiency that many pathologists recommend that anything that looks like a potassium deficiency get sent to a lab to be determined by a chemical analysis. These micronutrients all activate key enzymes responsible for controlling metabolic pathways, so the symptoms stem from a reduction in the consumption of elements, decreases in sugar production, and/or a halting of elements and sugars moving from point A to B.

When environmental conditions are within optimum range and there are micronutrients in your base grow or bloom nutrient solutions, you should rarely have to deal with micronutrient deficiencies, and overdoses will be even less frequent.

MAGNESIUM
Magnesium is a lightweight, silver-white alkali earth metal. It is a malleable metallic chemical element and is sometimes classified as a macronutrient. It is the most consumed of the micronutrients and is part of chlorophyll production. It's essential for photosynthesis. It also plays a role in activating many of the enzymes responsible for changes in growth and plant functions. It is present in organic matter, in dolomitic limestone, in fertilizers attached to other elements, and in chelated form.

IRON
Iron is a white, malleable metallic chemical element that can be easily magnetized. Iron is essential for chlorophyll formation and can easily become unavailable in alkaline (high pH) solutions, leading to chlorosis of new growth. Plants can absorb iron much easier in chelated form, even in alkaline conditions, and the elements attached are taken up along with it.

MOLYBDENUM
Named by K. W. Scheele in 1781 after its isolation by the Swedish chemist P. J. Hjelm, molybdenum is a hard, shiny, silver-white metallic chemical element. It is important for the processing of nitrogen inside of a plant. Molybdenum

Micronutrient deficiencies are rare, but this illustration shows a deficiency of magnesium.

Micronutrient deficiencies are rare, but this illustration shows a deficiency of iron.

deficiency can be difficult to diagnose because it will look like a mild nitrogen deficiency. In fertilizers, molybdenum is usually in the form of a salt and attached to another nutrient like potassium molybdate, but it can also be chelated to iron or aluminum.

CHLORINE
Chlorine was named in 1810 by Sir Humphrey Davy after he proved it to be an element. He named it after its yellow-green appearance. It is a poisonous, gaseous chemical element, is one of the halogens, and has a disagreeable odor. In fertilizers it is usually in chloride form, which is when it is combined with another element such as iron. Chlorine plays an important role in the rate at which plants can metabolize other nutrients, and while it is only taken up in small amounts, it impacts whether the plant can reach its genetic potential by allowing for consumption of elements at an increased rate.

MANGANESE
Usually hard and brittle, manganese is a grayish white metallic chemical element that rusts like iron but is not magnetic. It is used by enzyme systems to aid in breaking down carbohydrates and in nitrogen metabolism. These functions help keep a plant healthy and developing correctly throughout its life. Symptoms of a deficiency can appear similar to an iron deficiency, or spots of dead tissue may fall off, making the leaves appear ragged. Manganese is found in fertilizers in salt form, such as manganese chloride.

ZINC
Zinc is a bluish white metallic chemical element, usually found in combination with another element. Zinc is essential for sugar and carbohydrate use in plants. It regulates consumption, thus providing energy for chemical processes within plants. It also plays a role in the enzyme systems, assisting them in regulating plant growth. Deficiencies often appear as dwarfed leaves, sometimes with mottled or dead areas. A deficiency can also affect bud formation negatively. Zinc is included in fertilizers in the form of zinc oxide, zinc chelate, and the various zinc salts like zinc sulfate.

COPPER
In its elemental form, copper is reddish brown, malleable, ductile, and corrosion resistant. It conducts heat and electricity. It is included in fertilizers as a blue copper sulfate crystal sometimes called blue vitriol. Copper plays three important roles as a nutrient. It is used in the forming of reproductive growth and plays a background role in blooming, assists in the use of proteins for various chemical processes that involve growth, and works to assist in uptake at the root zone. Plants with copper deficiencies have leaves that appear bleached.

Micronutrient deficiencies are rare, but this illustration shows a deficiency of molybdenum.

Micronutrient deficiencies are rare, but this illustration shows a deficiency that may occur for zinc, copper, chlorine, or maganese.

Boron

Boron was named by Sir Humphrey Davey, who isolated it in 1808. Boron is a nonmetallic chemical element that occurs only in combination with other elements including oxygen, hydrogen, nitrogen, and silicon. It ranges in form from an amorphous brown powder to a brilliant hard crystal. In fertilizers it is found in the form of borax or is attached to another element. Boron assists in the use of other nutrients and acts as a regulator in plants. It aids in the production of carbohydrates and is essential for proper seed and fruit development. A boron deficiency can cause chlorosis in buds, dark spots on roots, and stems to crack.

Silicon

Named *Silicium* in 1808 by Sir Humphrey Davy, it was changed to silicon by Scotch chemist T. Thomson in 1817. It is a nonmetallic chemical element occurring in several forms. It is always in combination with another element and is more abundant in nature than any other element except oxygen. It is found in sand, quartz, opal, and chert, but it is sometimes used in fertilizers in its salt forms after being combined with other elements. Silicon helps plants build strong cell walls, making plants more resistant to insects and disease, and strengthens stems for better leaf positioning, improving photosynthesis. It also increases heat, drought, and cold tolerance and has become a popular supplement in nutrient solutions as a strengthener and preventative for all plants.

Sodium, Aluminum, and Cobalt

Sodium, aluminum, and cobalt play background roles, much like the other micronutrients, assisting in transpiration, cell construction, sugar transport use and regulation, activation of enzymes, and so forth. Sodium and aluminum are often present in base grow and bloom formulas as well as in micronutrient additive formulas or as water impurities. They can be obtained in organic or synthetic forms to add to your solution and meet your specific needs.

USING NUTRIENTS TO CREATE NUTRIENT SOLUTIONS

All of the macronutrients and micronutrients can be mixed together and used in various ways to feed your plants. The words *nutrient solution* is the broad name for the solution used to water the plants and in which all of the nutrients for plant growth are contained. Here are some ways that those nutrients and other elements can be combined to make the nutrient solution.

Supplements and Additives

Supplements and additives are fed to plants to bolster microbial activity at the root zone, increase size, improve flavor and aroma, correct deficiencies, improve health, aid in chemical processes, change growth patterns, ease or encourage change in growth stages, and flush plants of built-up nutrients.

A **supplement**, by definition, is something added to a nutrient solution to make up for a lack or deficiency.

An **additive** is something added to a nutrient solution to produce a desired effect.

Many manufacturers now package supplements and additives together in specific formulas that make them more effective in combination. Some supplements can be used like additives to cause specific effects (phosphorus and its ability to force blooming) and some additives can be used like supplements (vitamins and hormones). Because the definition of whether what you're using is a supplement or an additive can depend on your intentions and they are often found together in the same package, they will be listed together.

Macronutrients and Micronutrients as Additives and Supplements

The essential nutrients are the most common supplements, and the primary macronutrients are the most commonly used additives. It is easy to use them as a supplement to fix a deficiency once you have diagnosed which nutrient or nutrients are low in your solution.

Choose a source for that nutrient and calculate it into your feed chart as a supplement. Make an educated guess at how much to use to fix the problem or start with 1 millileter per liter of solution. If the desired correction is not achieved by the next reservoir change, go to 2 milliliter per liter and so on until corrected. Each macronutrient is unique when used as an additive or supplement.

NITROGEN

Usually a nitrogen additive is used to correct chlorosis during heavy blooming. It could be argued that this practice is really supplementing nitrogen since the yellowing associated with 4 to 6 weeks of heavy blooming is a deficiency, but since it isn't the norm to feed nitrogen at 3-week intervals during bloom, we will consider this use of nitrogen as an additive.

Using a liquid nitrogen source, add the equivalent of 1 milliliter per liter of a 5-0-0 rated nitrogen source to your reservoir at 3-week intervals. This should keep leaves nice and green throughout blooming. Any source can be used as long as the strength is the equivalent of 1 milliliter per liter of 5-0-0. If you are using a manufactured nitrogen additive, follow the manufacturer's instructions.

PHOSPHORUS

Phospholoading is the practice of using chelated phosphates to stop vertical growth, induce flowering, or encourage more bloom sites and larger flowers. This can be done at photoperiod change in one large dose, or throughout flowering in a smaller dose each reservoir change.

FEED CHARTS

The feed chart is a tool for formulating a plan of exactly how much of each ingredient is in the nutrient solution you will feed to your plants. The charts are normally broken down by reservoir cycles (10, 7, 5, and so forth). Each cycle will list the amount of each fertilizer, additive, or supplement in the solution. Typically, ounces or milliliters are used for the nutrient. This will be listed per gallon/liter or for the size of the reservoir; for example, 5 milliliters per gallon or 150 milliliters per 30-gallon reservoir.

It is common to see feed charts from fertilizer manufacturers broken down into weeks. This is the middle of the road for reservoir changes. If you use a manufacturer's feed chart and you want to have longer or shorter cycles, it shouldn't be a problem. Always use a meter to check PPM or EC, as these can lower as time goes by. An alternate method is to never go more than 14 days between checking levels. This is a good rule of thumb for the maximum life of a reservoir. Longer periods can create imbalances in the solution and lead to deficiencies. With that being said, the fertilizer manufacturers' feed charts are excellent tools. They follow the same basic rules of formulating a feed chart.

Creating a Feed Chart

The feed chart helps you track your nutrients—amounts, timing, and so forth. Start by making sure there is space to track all essential nutrients. Then evaluate the numbers.

- Are nutrients in the appropriate ratios for each developmental stage?
- Are nutrients in the appropriate amount (EC/PPM) for your irrigation technique and each developmental stage?
- Are additives and supplements included in ways that don't push the EC (PPM) to undesirable levels?

By following these same rules, you can create your own feeding chart with any group of fertilizers, supplements, and additives. If you started by making a nutrient checklist, you are halfway there. Everything you want to be present is accounted for, so the first rule is taken care of.

NUTRIENT CHECKLIST

Nutrients

Type	Source	N-P-K	Feeding Frequency
☐ Grow	_____	_____	_____
☐ Bloom	_____	_____	_____
☐ Micro	_____	_____	_____

Additives/Supplements

Type	Source	N-P-K	Feeding Frequency
☐ Hormones	_____	_____	_____
☐ Vitamins	_____	_____	_____
☐ Carbohydrates	_____	_____	_____
☐ Proteins	_____	_____	_____
☐ Microbiology	_____	_____	_____
☐ Bloom	_____	_____	_____
☐ Flush	_____	_____	_____

Products/Ingredients	Abbreviation	Cost
_____	_____	_____
_____	_____	_____
_____	_____	_____
_____	_____	_____
_____	_____	_____
_____	_____	_____
_____	_____	_____
_____	_____	_____
_____	_____	_____
_____	_____	_____
_____	_____	_____

Total: _____

There are several products that use these special chelated phosphate profiles. When using these products, be careful to feed less than the manufacturer's recommendations. I recommend feeding one half of what the label suggests. To guarantee the induction of flowering and prolific bloom sites, manufacturers usually suggest a mix so strong that your plants will have problems such as chlorosis, leaf scorch, and salt damage. Mix at half strength to avoid this and still get the desired effect from the additive or supplement.

POTASSIUM

Potassium sulfates and seaweed extracts are excellent sources of potassium. Potassium is used as an additive to strengthen a plant's structures, increase resistance to pathogens, and speed uptake of nutrients. It also aids in cellulose formation, photosynthesis, and rapid movement of carbohydrates through the vascular system, and it hardens flowers. When using a potassium additive, follow the manufacturer's recommendations. You can calculate the dosage based on the concentration of the potassium source and the stage of growth of your plant.

PHOSPHORUS AND POTASSIUM

Bloom boosters are potent mixtures of nonchelated phosphorus and potassium. They usually contain diverse P and K sources to provide the four results desired from bloom additives: boosters, accelerators, hardeners, and flower enhancers. They often contain micronutrients formulated to complement uptake, aid chemical processes, and stimulate enzymes and sugars associated with blooming and essential oil production of marijuana.

Most manufacturers recommend using these products from the beginning of flowering up to the flush phase. They are easy to spot on the retail shelf as they contain no nitrogen and have names like "Ginormous," "Beastie Bloomz," "Bloombastic," and so forth. Follow the manufacturer's recommendations for dosages.

CALCIUM, MAGNESIUM, AND IRON

The most common application of these nutrients is as a supplemental curative/corrective tonic to fix chlorosis. There are many products available that contain these three nutrients as their main ingredients with some other micronutrients that facilitate uptake and efficient use. They can be used individually or in their combined formulas as additives to promote healthier growth and thicker structures, increase stress and pathogen resistance, and help regulate chemical processes.

SILICON

Silicon can be added to your nutrient solution as a supplement to correct a silicon deficiency. It has become increasingly popular to use silicon as an additive to promote strong cellular growth that is pathogen resistant and heat and cold tolerant, and exhibits improved photosynthesis. Silicon formulas usually contain some potassium, but there are silicon-only formulas. Regardless of the formulation you use, follow the manufacturer's dosage instructions. Silicon is considerably effective at producing healthier, stronger plants, and using it is a good preventative measure against stress, bad environmental conditions, insects, and pathogens.

MICRONUTRIENT BLENDS

Hydroponic nutrient solutions need all the essential nutrients present to perform well. In traditional in-ground gardening, micronutrients are almost always present in sufficient amounts in the soil and the water used for irrigation, so they are not often added to fertilizers specifically designed for soil application.

Make sure you are familiar with the contents of your grow or bloom solution and note the presence or absence of every micronutrient. If they are listed as an afterthought at the end of the ingredients listing or as "trace elements," it is a good idea to use a specifically formulated micronutrient blend to make sure you aren't missing anything. If your grow or bloom solution says that it contains "all the essential nutrients" or "all the trace elements," then it should have all the micronutrients you will need. Most fertilizers formulated for hydroponic applications have a good amount of micronutrients, but it is up to you to always be aware of your ingredients. Some are only macronutrient blends designed to be used with a micronutrient blend. Micronutrients are used as supplements to correct deficiencies and as additives to bolster almost every chemical process involved in plant growth and development.

Hormones

Plant hormones are organic substances made in small amounts by plants that are moved to specific locations in plants where they control growth and development processes. There are five known plant hormones that control everything, including type of growth and development, growth and development structure, speed of growth and development, cell elongation and division, and regulation and production of enzymes, as well as fruit ripening, stomata function, leaf and flower senescence, and abscission. They work together, and the amount of each one that is present or absent in an area of the plant determines growth and development processes.

HORMONES AND THEIR FUNCTIONS

- **Abscisic acid:** Makes stomata close and is located in high concentrations in leaves, stems, and green fruit
- **Auxin:** Controls cell elongation, is key in plants moving toward light (phototropism) in response to gravity (geotropism) and strong vertical

growth from a single meristem (apical dominance). It also controls ethylene production and fruit development and is the hormone applied to clones to get them to root. IAA is the form of auxin produced in plants. NAA and 2,4D are synthetic auxin-like compounds. Auxin is found in high concentrations in seeds, young leaves, and the tips of vertical growth (meristems of apical buds).

- **Cytokinin:** Controls cell division, makes plants grow bushier (axillary bud growth), helps shoots grow, and delays leaves from yellowing and falling. Cytokinin is made in the root zone and transported to organs.
- **Ethylene:** Controls the ripening of fruit leaves and flowering aging and falling. It is located in high concentrations in fruit tissues, aged leaves and flowers, and the nodes of stems.
- **Gibberellin:** Controls shoot lengthening, bolting, and flowering in biennials and certain enzymes in specific plant species. Gibberellin is found in high concentrations in vertically growing buds and roots, young leaves, and seeds.

The five hormones can be found individually in specific supplements and additives to improve function of the mixtures or all together with vitamins as a multipurpose activator, reviver, and growth stimulator.

Auxins can be found in root drenches and stimulators, or with gibberellin in specialized fertilizers and growth enhancers.

Abscisic acid is sometimes used with silicon and potassium additives.

Cytokinin can be found in bloom booster and additives designed for flowering and fruit enhancement.

Plants can absorb hormones at their roots and use them immediately for key functions, store them for use in times of stress, or to eventually spur developmental changes.

Feeding plants hormones through their roots became popular during World War II to improve agriculture in the United States and help with the war effort. The discoveries and formula of the Vitamin Institute are highly acclaimed to this day and still sold in the same formula as Superthrive in garden shores and retail outlets. By combining vitamins with hormones, the Vitamin Institute made a product that can achieve remarkable growth, higher yield, and a high level of stress resistance. You can add Superthrive to your nutrient solution at a rate of 1 tablespoon to 15 gallons just before each change in growth stage, as a root drench or dip when transplanting, as stress occurs, or for your plant's entire life to promote health, vigor, and development and combat stress. Because many vitamins are acidic and Superthrive contains a huge amount of concentrated vitamins, it can lower the pH of your solution quite a bit. Test the pH of the solution and use an alkaline substance to bring the solution back into optimal range if necessary.

Vitamins

Vitamins are complex organic substances sometimes produced in plants that are essential in small amounts for the regulation of the metabolism, growth, and other chemical functions. Plants can also absorb vitamins at the root zone. Most plants produce enough of the necessary vitamins to survive and reproduce.

Feeding vitamins as an additive has become popular for a lot of reasons. Having additional vitamins available allows for valuable energy to be expended elsewhere in times of stress, developmental change, or accelerated growth, and plants can use more vitamins than they produce.

A vitamins, B vitamins (especially B1-thiamine), and E vitamins are popular and can be found in a lot of synthetic and organic nutrients, supplements, and additives. P vitamins (bioflavonoid) are sometimes found in carbohydrate formulas and flushes. There are more than fifty different vitamins that benefit plants in pretty amazing ways! There have been experiments showing that some trees, for example, can grow at twice the speed of genetic copies that are not fed vitamins and hormones. You will find specific vitamins in most additives. These are usually the specific vitamins that have been isolated to aid the chemical processes associated with that additive. For a performance boost, as a preventative treatment for stress, and to bolster developmental changes, you can use products specifically labeled to have certain effects. Be aware that these products affect pH or contain macronutrients, so you may need to make other adjustments when using them.

Carbohydrates

Carbohydrates are organic compounds belonging to the saccharide groups and include starches, cellulose, and sugars. Plants produce carbohydrates and use them as a source of energy for major plant functions like growth, development, resisting stress and pathogens, and oil production (which is key to marijuana growing). Plants store excess carbohydrates in "nutrient sinks" around the plant—the petiole (leaf stem) is one carbohydrate sink—and use them as necessary.

The link between stress and the level of sugar in petiole tissue is so strong, horticulturalists can tell if a plant is using its sugar to fight stress before the plant shows any visible symptoms. This is done by measuring the concentration of sugar in a drop of liquid squeezed from petiole tissue using a sugar refractometer. Sugar refractometers measure brix, which is the sugar density or concentration named after nineteenth-century German chemist A. F. Brix. They measure up to around 30 percent, which is almost one-third pure carbohydrates, and would indicate a very healthy, well-fed plant. By monitoring the concentration of sugar periodically for large drops, stresses can be detected before they damage plant structures and divert large amounts of energy away from key chemical processes to counteract the stress. A drop of 8 percent or more is a good indicator that something is causing extra energy to be used.

Plants can absorb extra carbohydrates at their root zone, first using carbs to fuel chemical processes, then storing extra in nutrient sinks for later use.

Carbohydrates are popular as an additive because they directly affect fruit size, taste, and essential oil content. More carbohydrates present means larger fruit and more essential oils. Carbohydrates and specific esters, amino acids, organic acids, and vitamins can increase taste profiles or alter them altogether. Feeding extra, specialized carbs has become known as "carbo loading" and can be done at the beginning of flowering, throughout the flowering phase, for the entirety of the plant's life, or during the flush just before harvest. Look for specific products formulated for this purpose.

Most carbohydrate additives have specific profiles. The sweet line is designed to impart a specific background flavor in fruit and essential oils, while products like Wet Betty kick up the production of a specific carbohydrate used to produce terpenes and essential oils, giving plants more of their natural flavor, aroma, and higher oil content. Follow the manufacturer's instructions for dosage with these products.

Proteins, Enzymes, and Acids

Proteins are a large class of complex compounds of amino acid chains bound with peptides. These chains are connected to each other by nucleic acid, lipids, and other constituents. Proteins are found in all cells and function in the form of enzymes, hormones, or antibodies. Enzymes are proteins formed in plant cells or made synthetically that act as organic catalysts in initiating or speeding up chemical reactions. Plants use proteins to build cells and start the chemical reactions that lead to plant growth, nutrient use, nutrient transport, and developmental changes. Plants also use proteins to fight pathogens in the form of antibodies and to combine elements in a solution to make them more accessible to plants. If you see a capital *L* before a protein's name, that means it is one of the left-handed special arrangement proteins. It is asymmetrical in atomic structure and performs a specific role in a nutrient's use in a plant.

Proteins, enzymes, and L-acids are present in a lot of nutrients, supplements, and additives. They are popular additions to nutrient solutions to kick-start growth and development and aid in pathogen destruction. They are produced by plants and used internally, but plants can greatly benefit from being fed extra proteins, enzymes, and acids. They are taken up in the root zones and moved around the plant. Specific proteins, enzymes, and acids can be found in additives to aid in their performance. They are available in synthetic forms and available in organic forms such as humic acid derived from leonardite or other ancient sea floor sources, worm castings, compost teas, and seaweed extracts. If they are present in an additive or supplement, they will be listed in the ingredients. If you are using a specific concentrated form, follow the manufacturer's dosage instructions.

Microbiology

Mycorrhizal fungi live in symbiosis with plant roots by infecting them, living off the carbon exuded by the roots, and breaking down organic matter and large complex nutrients, making them easier to absorb, and then moving the nutrients to exchange sites where they essentially trade them with the plants for carbon. Some species form protective water-storing sheaths around roots, while others spread out and greatly extend the mass of root zones.

There are many mycorrhizal inoculants on the market, some containing ten or more different species. They are a popular additive for organic solutions and hybrid (organic/synthetic blend) solutions. They have a harder time existing in a synthetic solution as the highly available nitrates can damage them, but more resistant strains can be purchased that will survive long enough to inoculate your root zone. An alternate application for synthetic solutions is to use them as a root dip. Take a newly rooted clone and dip it in a solution of the inoculant and water, then transplant to your medium of choice and feed a half-strength solution for 5 to 10 days to allow the fungi to take hold. The tougher strains should be established enough to survive in most synthetic solutions after that.

Trichoderma are mycoparasites, which means they eat fungi for nutrients. They establish themselves in the root zone and hang out waiting for a preferred food source to come along and become dinner. Not a whole lot is known about exactly how *Trichoderma* work to help plants grow, but it is known that certain strains such as T-22 can reduce a plant's need for nitrogen by up to 40 percent. *Trichoderma* are effective root zone defenders, at least from fungi, and are now in a lot of mycorrhizal inoculants to form a tag team of beneficial microbiology.

Beneficial bacteria can be added to your solution in the form of an inoculant, organic compost, or a worm tea component. They can also have a hard time in a nitrate-rich solution, but the high oxygen content of a reservoir does help aerobic bacterial species cope. There are some new nitrate-resistant species available commercially in hydroponics shops. The aerobic bacteria consume organic matter or other solution components and exude them as organic components that can be beneficial to root zones, feeding beneficial fungi and helping to strengthen them, which in turn feed plants.

The rhizobacteria can be used as well. They live in root zones and excrete gibberellin, cytokinin, and enzymes that roots can take up. They also produce chitinase, a substance that helps the beneficial fungi build larger, stronger walls. Rhizobacteria also help with nutrient uptake and, together with mycorrhizal fungi and *Trichoderma*, form a team that defend the root zone of the plant and make it work more efficiently.

Flushes and Hydrogen Peroxide

A common practice in cannabis culture is to flush plants with clean water for 5 to 10 days before harvest to push carbohydrates and other elements used in flavor production out of nutrient sinks and into flowers, terpenes, and trichomes. A good flush is one of the keys to a great final product. There are carbohydrate additives that are formulated to assist this process without leaving undesirable elements behind. Look for products with specific carbohydrates to impart background flavor profiles such as grape, citrus, piña colada, blueberry, and so forth. If this is not what you're looking for, use a product that is designed to bring forward the natural flavors.

There are also isotonic drenches that can be used to chemically unbind undesired elements, or used to treat excess salts in a medium after extended use or very heavy salt-based feeding cycles. To use as a flush additive before harvest, mix a reservoir with clean water and the isotonic drench to the manufacturer's specifications, run for 5 days, and then flush with clean water for 5 to 10 additional days.

Hydrogen peroxide is an older additive, but it is still unparalleled in combating aggressive algae and fungal infections of growing media. Add 1 capful to your reservoir and watch for 5 days to see if algae or fungus is gone. If it is, mix up a new reservoir; if not, double the strength and go again. There are still plant-specific H_2O_2 formulas available that contain some other ingredients that assist root zones. These products can be used as regular additives in synthetic nutrient solutions to clean and assist in uptake, and they can make root growth healthy, strong, and large. They immediately kill all microbiology, so don't use them in organic or hybrid solutions except as a last resort to save your plants. You can also mix them with clean water to use them as a transplant drench.

FORMULATING A NUTRIENT SOLUTION

Now that you understand all of the component parts to a nutrient solution, you can formulate your own.

To achieve your desired results, you need to make sure all the macronutrients and micronutrients are present in the amounts necessary to produce those results. You'll add more nitrogen for growth and more phosphorus and potassium for blooming.

There are two main categories of nutrient solutions: "grow" and "bloom." These are used with two different photoperiods: 24 hours (or 18/6) for "grow" and 12 hours of light for "bloom."

Fortunately for you, almost every fertilizer manufacturer has already done the initial formulation, preparation, and packaging of the fertilizers you will use as a base to provide the nutritional necessities and divided them into grow and bloom for you. You just have to decide whether to use them "straight up" or to tweak them. Here's how to formulate a nutrient solution.

Step 1: Design the base nutrient solution

Step 1 can be as complicated as mixing your own desired macronutrients into a custom formula or as simple as checking the label of a one-part complete fertilizer to make sure everything is present. Most high-end fertilizers are separated into two (or even three) parts, usually an A and B, but one-part fertilizers are gaining popularity. Always check the label and make sure all the essential nutrients are present; if they're not, find a supplement that contains the missing nutrients and round out your solution.

Step 2: Determine desired supplements for entire growth cycle
Decide what supplements and/or additives you would like to use for the entirety of the plant's life. Carbohydrates and silicon are popular, as are vitamins and hormones.

Step 3: Determine desired supplements for "grow" stage
Decide what supplements and/or additives you want to use for the vegetation or "grow" stage of your plant's life. Supplemental nitrogen, vitamins, hormones, low- to mid-range doses of carbohydrates, and silicon are all popular.

Step 4: Determine desired supplements for "bloom" stage
Consider what supplements and/or additives you will want to use during the flowering or "bloom" stage of your plant's life. High phosphorus and potassium bloom boosters, vitamins, hormones, and mid- to high-range doses of carbohydrates and silicon are popular.

Step 5: Determine desired supplements for specific times of growth cycle
Decide if you will be using any timed techniques or applications of specific supplements or additives and the dosage of these; for example: a nitrogen supplement every third week of flowering to maintain lush green leaves, phospholoading at photoperiod change, chemical induction of flowering during the last week of vegetation, timed vitamin and/or hormone applications, and the ever-popular final flush before harvest.

Step 6: Plot everything on the nutrient checklist provided for you
See page 139. This will give you a chance to double-check everything and will be a reference for total cost.

Step 7: Mix the solution
Pour 1 gallon of clean water in a bucket and mix up your solution to check pH and EC. Always keep your pH in optimum range and your EC below 4. Mix a bucket for "grow," a bucket for "bloom," and a bucket for every timed application to make sure pH and EC are correct. Record the data to check later. If you are following the manufacturer's dosage instructions for each product, this shouldn't be a problem. If pH is off, it can be adjusted using a base to raise it, or an acid to lower it. EC can be lowered by using slightly less of the "grow" or "bloom" base fertilizer.

MIXING A NUTRIENT SOLUTION

Once you've decided what will be in the nutrient solution, you can mix it. Follow these steps and you shouldn't have any problems with pH, EC, or nutrient fallout. Fallout is when a nutrient comes into contact with another nutrient with which it combines and forms a solid precipitate that is not accessible to plant roots.

Step 1: Fill the reservoir

Decide how many gallons of clean water you are going to put in your reservoir. For this example we will use a 30-gallon reservoir. Fill your reservoir with the clean water. Place your air stone in the reservoir and watch for the bubbling that signifies proper oxygen levels. Use tepid water or allow the water to reach 70 to 80 °F (tepid) before continuing.

Step 2: Calculate the nutrient formulas

Following the manufacturer's instructions for dose, calculate how much of your base "grow" or "bloom" solution to use with this equation: amount of fertilizer per gallon/liter × the number of gallons/liters in your reservoir. If your base fertilizer is a two- or three-part formula, read the dosage instructions carefully. Generally, two-part formulas will be equal, and three-part mixtures will be broken into a "grow" dosage and a "bloom" dosage.

Step 3: Mix the base fertilizer into the solution

Add the base fertilizer to your solution and mix it in. Always add in this order: K-P-N. This will keep the more reactive potassium and phosphate concentrations from coming into contact with nitrogen before they are diluted. Two-part fertilizers are almost always part A nitrogen heavy, and part B phosphate and potassium heavy. So add part B first, and then add part A to avoid any nutrients binding together into solids and "falling out" to the bottom of the reservoir. Clean the measuring cup or syringe in between measuring each part. If any concentrated fertilizer comes in contact with your hands, wash them before handling the next part. Concentrated fertilizers coming into contact with your skin can cause irritation or mild chemical burn, so be clean, safe, and careful.

Step 4: Calculate and add micronutrient dosages

If you're using a micronutrient supplement or additive, calculate the dosage (fertilizer per gallon × the gallons of water in the reservoir) and add it, making sure to mix the reservoir by stirring the water for a minute, or just leave a submersible pump running during the entire process so that it stirs the water for you. Continue this process with each individual supplement or additive you wish to add to the reservoir.

Step 5: Mix

After all ingredients are calculated and mixed into the clean water in the reservoir, allow your pump to stir them for 3 minutes or more, or hand-stir for a minute or so, until you are comfortable everything is mixed well and that nothing is solidified.

Step 6: Check and adjust pH and EC

Calibrate your measurement equipment according to the manufacturer's instructions. Check pH and EC using your measurement equipment after it has been calibrated. Adjust pH if necessary and check it again, repeating this step until pH measures at the desired level.

Step 7: Feed

Place your lid on the reservoir (optional) and begin the irrigation cycle.

Vegetative (Grow) Stage

Decide how long to grow in the vegetative stage. Cycle 1 should be around 1EC (500 PPM) and the N-P-K ratio should be nitrogen dominant. Cycles 2 and 3 should have the same N-P-K ratio, but EC (PPM) should steadily increase, bridging the gap between the requirements of a young plant and a plant in the third stage of vegetative growth. By cycle 4, you should be at full strength with an EC around 3 (1500 PPM).

You will notice on most fertilizer manufacturers' feed charts that every cycle after you have reached full strength remains the same until flowering is initiated. On all the example charts, an asterisk (*) will appear on these full-strength cycles. If you want a longer vegetation or flowering period, continue repeating these as many weeks as desired.

If you have a chemical induction cycle before photoperiod change, it will be the final cycle in your grow period. The EC of this cycle should be equal to the full-strength vegetation cycle. This prevents unnecessary stress and deficiencies. The N-P-K ratio may differ slightly depending on your preference, but it should be phosphorus dominant. More potassium is commonly fed during these cycles to prevent stress and facilitate biochemical processes. This cycle concludes your vegetation period.

Flowering (Bloom) Stage

For the flowering period, change the photoperiod to the appropriate amount of darkness (12 hours for short-day plants). Cycle 1 of flowering should continue with a phosphorus dominant N-P-K ratio and the same EC (PPM) as the full-strength vegetation cycle. Cycle 2 of flowering should have a slightly higher EC (0.2 or 0.3/ 100–150 PPM). This will facilitate more flowering sites, larger flowers, and faster development. Cycle 3 will typically be full strength for flowering. EC (PPM) should be slightly higher than cycle 2 (again .2 or .3/ 100–150 PPM higher). To finish, continue repeating cycle 3 of flowering until the flush period.

Flush Period

The flush period should begin either at peak ripeness or just before. If you have a plant that takes 9 weeks to mature and your cycles are 7 days, then your flush will begin at cycle 10. Flushes can be a two-cycle-long reduction in EC (PPM), an immediate reduction to clean water, or a carbohydrate-only cycle. With a two-cycle reduction you reduce the EC to what it was at the beginning of flowering for flush cycle 1. By reducing EC (PPM) you effectively ease the plant into flush. Cycle 2 of the flush period should have an EC (PPM) around 0.5 (250 PPM). An alternate two-cycle flushing technique is to use an isotonic drench for cycle 1 to break free nutrients and flush them away. Cycle 2 should then be clean water or a carbohydrate additive. This will fill fruit bodies with sugar from their nutrient sinks and from the roots, increasing flavor or altering the flavor profile. One-cycle flushes of just clean water are very effective in moving sugars from nutrient sinks to flowers and fruit. This technique is cheap and effective and will most likely remain popular. Some other flushing techniques include two cycles of clean water, one cycle of carbohydrates only, one cycle drench with one cycle water, and one cycle clean water with one cycle carbohydrates.

Real-Time Data

It is a good idea to keep a second feed chart to record any deviations from the original plan. Each cycle, start with a blank chart and fill it out by hand just after you change your solution. Record the solution's contents and list any notes on deficiencies and plant performance by date. This information can be extremely useful in formulating future feed charts.

The following examples of feed charts all follow the same basic rules. There is a checklist and chart representing each of the popular types of solutions. The Hesi Hydro formula is a synthetic commercial fertilizer with timed additives. It is designed for any medium and irrigation technique. Hesi Coco is a similar formula, except it is designed specifically for coco coir. The Nature's Nectar formula is a certified organic formula with additives by Higrocorp. The Nature's Nectar and Organa additives are listed with OMRI. This solution is changed every 5 days and works best without forced air in the reservoir. It may not work well in deep water culture or aeroponic irrigation systems. It is designed to be used with any medium. The General Organics formula is vegan, meaning it contains only organic ingredients that aren't derived from animals. It isn't OMRI listed, but the vegan fertilizers usually aren't. It is formulated for any medium and irrigation technique. The General Organics solution works best with aeration in the form of large bubbles so, air stones aren't necessary. The Dutch Master formulas are hybrid solutions using specialized organic and synthetic ingredients. The ingredients are laboratory grade and prepared with an ionic charge for maximum effectiveness. The standard formula is designed for timed-drip systems, NFT, and aeroponics. The aggressive formula is designed

FEED CHART #1

Product	1	2	3	4	5	6	7	8	9	10	11	12	13	14	15	16	17

FEED CHART #2

Product	Grow				Bloom				Flush	
	1	2	3	4	1	2	3	4	1	2

for heavy-feeding plants in the previously listed systems or for subirrigation, constant drip irrigation, and deep water culture. Dutch Master is designed to be used with any medium and irrigation technique. The final formula is an example of how to use timed additives, constant additives, and a base fertilizer all together. It is suitable for any medium and irrigation technique.

The next step, now that you know how to set up a system and create a nutrient solution, is to learn about the production techniques used to grow a healthy and robust crop of marijuana.

CHAPTER 8

Production Techniques

The way you move plants through the stages of growth is called "production." This chapter focuses on the techniques you can use to manage your plants.

Several factors determine the production techniques you'll use, including:

- Desired harvest frequency
- Plant size and structure
- Available space
- Budget
- Amount of time available to manage the plants

The production techniques described build upon all of the information in other chapters, including growing media, circulation, watering techniques, and nutrient mixes and feeding schedules. Production is where everything comes together.

There are two types of production techniques described here: production techniques based on the place in which the production is happening (chambers) and techniques that relate to plant care during production (trellising, staking, bending, and re-vegging).

Opposite: Doing clean, careful work is the key to all production techniques, and plant management in general.

PRODUCTION CHAMBERS
Single Chamber
This is the simplest technique and has been a favorite of professionals, enthusiasts, and home growers since the beginning of hydroponics and indoor gardening. Because of its flexibility in terms of plant size and type, low cost, low man-hour requirements, and ease of use, it will likely remain popular indefinitely.

HOW IT WORKS
You, the grower, place plants in the growing environment and grow them in the vegetative state for the desired amount of time. Then you induce flowering with a photoperiod change (by changing the length of the light and dark cycles in the growing environment). As long as you plan for the plants to grow (have sufficient height) and stretch, you won't have to move the lights until it is time to harvest. After harvest, you'll start over with new plants, change the photoperiod back to what you need for vegetative growth, and begin again.

CALCULATING CYCLES
To calculate yearly harvest, time a cycle in days, then divide 364 by that number. For example, 60 days for a cycle would yield 6 yearly harvests (364 divided by 60 = 6), with 1 extra day to harvest.

Staggered Chambers
This is the technique of building multiple growing environments and staggering the planting schedule to multiply your harvests. You can build as many chambers as you want and stagger plants in them according to whichever schedule works best for you; just keep in mind the increased cost in electricity, workload, and equipment that adding multiple chambers brings. It is a good idea to schedule reservoir changes on the same day to avoid overworking yourself.

HOW IT WORKS
If you have a species that takes 90 days to mature, but you want to harvest new product every 45 days, you would construct two growing environments (chambers) and plant them 45 days apart, harvesting and replanting each every time a cycle finishes. This entails twice the work as one chamber and a budget twice the size, but gives you eight harvests a year.

CALCULATING CYCLES
Divide the number of days your species takes to fully mature by the number of chambers you have to calculate the number of days between plantings to space them out evenly. For example, if you have three chambers, you can plant a 90-day crop every 30 days. To calculate the number of annual yields, divide 364 by this number (364 divided by 30 days = 12).

This allows you to harvest twice as many times a year. For example, 364 days divided by 60 days (the length of time it takes to finish a plant in the flowering chamber) = 6 (the number of harvests per year) and gives you the advantage of static environmental conditions. Many growers use their vegetative chamber to grow enough plants to fill two or even three flowering chambers because plants are smaller during early developmental stages and can be packed tighter during vegetative growth. Using multiple flowering chambers greatly increases the volume of harvest at one time because more plants growing at the same time equals more product to harvest at the same time.

You could grow enough plants in the vegetative chamber and fill 3 flowering chambers every 6 weeks, tripling the size of your yield. That is, 364 days in a year divided by 60 days in a flowering period = 6 yearly harvests from 3 flowering chambers instead of 1. The increase in yield by vegetating enough plants in 1 chamber to fill 3 flowering chambers is substantial.

Dedicated Chambers

This is the technique of building chambers and designating their use for vegetation or flowering. It is a popular way to increase the number of yields per year. Let's say you have two 8×4×7 chambers built, your species takes 90 days to finish (mature), and each plant requires 4 square feet of space just before harvest. You would grow the plants for 6 weeks in a vegetative state and 6 weeks in a flowering state.

HOW IT WORKS

Your first step is to designate one chamber as the vegetation environment. Adjust the environmental conditions in this chamber to the desired temperature (75°F, RH, relative humidity between 55 percent to 65 percent) and photoperiod (either 24 hours lights on or 18 hours lights on/6 hours lights off).

Designate the other chamber as the flowering environment and adjust the environmental conditions to the desired temp, RH, and photoperiod 12 hours of light and 12 hours of dark. The lights in the flowering chamber can be left off to conserve electricity until plants are ready to be moved into it from the vegetation chamber.

CALCULATING CYCLES

Plant 8 plants in the vegetative chamber and allow them to grow for 6 weeks, then move them to the flowering chamber and plant 8 new plants in the vegetative chamber. This allows you to harvest twice as many times a year. For example, 365 days divided by 42 days (the length of time it takes to finish a plant in the flowering chamber) = 8 (the number of harvests per year) and gives you the advantage of static environmental conditions. Using multiple flowering chambers greatly increases the volume of harvest at one time because more plants growing at the same time equals more product to harvest at the same time.

You could grow 24 plants in the vegetative chamber and fill 3 flowering chambers every 6 weeks, tripling the size of your yield. That is, 364 days in a year divided by 42 days in a flowering period = 8 yearly harvests from 3 flowering chambers instead of 1. The increase in yield by vegetating enough plants in 1 chamber to fill 3 flowering chambers is substantial.

PLANT CARE PRODUCTION TECHNIQUES

Plant care production techniques are primarily aimed at fitting more plant in less space and growing more buds for harvest. The key to higher production is more branching, and these techniques will get you there.

Vertical Trellising

Vertical trellising is the method of providing support for plants using a stake or cage. The trellis itself is oriented vertically, parallel to the stem of the plant. Most plants will grow on their own without a stake to hold them up. When you start pruning a plant to encourage more side growth, however, and the plant becomes heavier, a vertical trellis system becomes necessary to prevent plants from falling over and breaking.

The point of trellising when growing marijuana is to allow the grower to manipulate auxin levels in the plant. Reminder: auxin is the hormone produced in the apical meristem (top growing point) of all plants. This hormone inhibits side branching. When you remove its apical meristem, a plant will produce more lateral branches. You can use this trellising and pruning technique to begin a mother plant.

Bending

Bending plant stems means exactly what it sounds like. You bend the main plant stem at a 90-degree angle. This causes changes in auxin levels along the plant stem and results in branching. Because you did not remove the main growing tip, though, it will continue to grow vertically. If you continue to bend the supple new growth horizontally as it reaches up to grow vertically, you can achieve two things:

1. You can fit a much larger plant into a smaller area. For example, a plant grows 1 foot vertically; you bend it so it stretches horizontally to the right 1 foot. Let it grow up 4 inches and then bend it so it stretches horizontally left for 1 foot. Then repeat this process two more times. You can now fit a 6-foot-tall plant into 2 square feet of space.
2. You change the hormone balance in the plant to encourage growth of more flowering sites, meaning a bigger harvest.

TRELLIS-STAKE-BEND

Vertical trellising

Horizontal
trellising

Bending

SEA OF GREEN (SOG) AND SCREEN OF GREEN (SCROG)

SOG

SCROG

Horizontal Trellising

Horizontal trellising is a technique that is more specific to indoor gardening, but is becoming more popular. The cut-flower industry uses it in order to support more plants with less work.

This production technique involves stretching a net or trellis suspended horizontally over the plant (or plants) so that the plants can grow up through the trellis. You can tie the plants to the net/trellis for structural support or bend the plants into the net to maximize space and increase yield.

When you combine bending with horizontal trellising and arrange lights to shine on the plants from the top and sides, you can increase yields significantly. It is also a way to get more out of each individual plant, but you make a trade in time to harvest because you'll need more time to work with your plants and bend the vegetative growth into a thick horizontal wall that can then sprout flowering buds.

CREATING A HORIZONTAL WALL

Step 1: Determine the growing zone by using the back of your hand to measure the temperature below the light. Place your hand under the lamp and raise your hand closer to the light until it is uncomfortable. This is the top of your growing zone. Decide how tall you want your plants to be (18 to 24 inches is good).

Step 2: Place the horizontal trellis securely in your growing environment by attaching four poles to the walls of your growth chamber, extending poles up from the irrigation system, or constructing a new frame. Stretch the trellis net and make sure it is nice and taut. It will be supporting some of the weight of your plants and you don't want it to droop in the middle.

Step 3: Place the plants in the irrigation system underneath the trellis and grow them in a vegetative state until they grow up through the trellis.

Step 4: When the plants reach a height of 4 to 6 inches above the trellis, begin bending them back down underneath square openings in the trellis.

Step 5: Keep repeating Step 4, bending the plants until they have formed a horizontal living wall. Popular bending patterns include:

- Spirals, left to right or right to left
- Blocks (like the example used earlier to describe bending)
- Alternate rows (where plants are placed alternately on both sides of the environment and bent in straight lines opposite where they are located across the trellis)

Step 6: Induce flowering with a photoperiod change, chemically, or by phospholoading, if stretch is a key factor with your species. (Learn how to do this in Chapter 7, the nutrients chapter.)

Step 7: As flowering proceeds, be attentive to your light placement and be ready to raise it if necessary to avoid burning the tops of your flowers.

The effect you should get will look like a sheet of tightly packed, robust, vibrant flowers, fed from a low number of thick, healthy stalks. With some creativity and good planning, you can use this technique with any of the basic production methods.

You can also prune your plants so they have a bushier structure. Then allow them to grow into a horizontal trellis, tying them for support or bending to maximize space. Treat each branch the same as you would a whole plant, bending down into an adjacent square when it is 4 to 6 inches above the trellis.

Staking

Staking is bending without a trellis and is popular for the same reasons—increasing branching—as well as for shortening normally tall plants. You can stake a plant in many different ways. You can use some string and a tent stake—tying the string around the stake, then the plant, and bending the plant stem so that it is pulled over horizontally (take care not to break the plant). Then drive the stake into the ground or the container, holding the plant down. You can use just about anything that can accomplish this: a stake, a pole, PVC, croquet loops, or even a rock, as long as the plant bends horizontally and stays that way.

The same things that happen during bending also occur during staking: an attempt to return to vertical growth, more flowering sites, and train more vertical growth for more flowering sites.

Combination Techniques

You can use the trellising, staking, and bending techniques together to achieve higher yields.

One example is staking and bending. Prune the plant as desired and, as horizontal braches begin to grow vertically, stake them down to train the plant to widen more, and you'll get the same effect.

When your plants are growing, you'll encounter different pest and disease problems. Chapter 9 discusses how to deal with these and keep your plants healthy.

Integrated Pest Management and Troubleshooting

While cannabis is generally considered a strong plant with many inherent resistances to fungus and disease, it is also a likely candidate for attack from pests because it's fast-growing and moves lots of nutrients and water, which makes it an ideal food source for most sucking insects.

Without its natural defense of sticky pubescent structures that contain chemical compounds that work as insecticides, cannabis might never have made it to the modern era. The fact that those same structures contain chemicals that benefit man undoubtedly led to the spread of the plant from Asia to where it's now being cultivated around the world. It should also be noted that the taller plants from the Black Sea region have also spread across the world but primarily for their textile and industrial purposes. Outdoors in a temperate environment, a cannabis plant can grow freely provided it gets adequate water and nutrients. In a stand of one hundred properly placed plants, you may lose fewer than 3 percent annually to pests, fungus, and disease.

The number one problem indoor growers have is pest infestation, so that is what this chapter primarily covers. Fungal infection is definitely a secondary issue, due to circulation and humidity associated with indoor growing. Instances of viral attack in an indoor setting are rare.

Opposite: Even indoors, some pests (primarily insects) can find their way to your plants.

FUNGAL INFECTION

Fungus floats in the air, grows in moisture-rich environments, and can be carried on clothes and tools. Keep your growing environment as close to the optimal 75°F and 50 percent RH. This should prevent formation of conditions hospitable to fungal spores. Avoid foliar feeding late into flowering without adequate air circulation to help ripening flowers dry and stay dry. If fungus is a persistent issue or if you get a clone from someone and it has a persistent fungus, inexpensive soaps and/or neem oil will control it. In a large growing setup with huge buds packed close together, use horticultural oil to control fungus. Common fungus problems include cucurbit powdery mildew, forms of botrytis, and blackspot on damaged leaves.

DEALING WITH PESTS

The first defense against pest infestation is prevention. Growing from seed is a sure way to avoid pests in an environment you build yourself. By wearing clean clothes and using clean tools when you garden, as well as following good cultural practices, most of these issues can be avoided.

It can be advantageous to use a clone produced by someone else because you can skip the sexing process and may even have an idea of what you're going to get for the final product, but using plant material from others is the most common source of pest infestations for indoor growers. You should always quarantine (keep separate from existing plants) new plants for 10 days or more when receiving them from an outside source. Spray them every 5 days with a pyrethrin-based insecticide. Spray at the end of your light cycle so the plants can dry in the dark. This will minimize leaf damage from the spray. If your cycle is running 24 hours, just allow them to dry in the dark. If there are no signs of pests after this period, it is probably safe to introduce the clone into your environment.

Integrated Pest Management

Integrated Pest Management (IPM) is the name given to the practice of using a combination of tactics to keep pests from ruining a crop. These IPM tactics might or might not include chemical control, depending on the preference of each gardener. Nonchemical pest control tactics include cultural, mechanical, and biological controls as well as good sanitary practices. Most of these tactics are used as preventive measures in an attempt to prevent pest infestations from happening. Sometimes, even with preventative measures, certain conditions can still allow a pest population to build up to injurious levels. If pests do build up, you can use other control methods to reduce the population of the pest and rescue the crop.

When examining plants, it is important to look at them *closely*. By looking closely, you will be able to see the egg masses, small larvae, or early stages of damage that are present before damage becomes excessive. Pests can be found on the undersides of leaves, on top of leaves, on stems, in stems, in buds, or on roots. Examine all parts of the plant, even if they are not parts that will be harvested, because pests attacking or weakening any part of the plant will affect the final product.

From a foot away, this mass of eggs could go unnoticed.

Control Measures

When you think of pest control, you might think of immediately getting out the sprays. That's not necessarily what you need to do. There are three types of control options available: mechanical control, biological control, and chemical control.

MECHANICAL CONTROL

Make traps that attract an insect by color (usually yellow or white) using colored cards covered with a sticky substance, or setting out colored bowls filled with soapy water. Other traps use a scent or "pheromone" to attract the pest to a sticky surface or an enclosure. Do not rely on traps such as these to control insects in an open area, but rather use them more as an indicator of a pest's presence.

In addition to traps, mechanical control also includes simply removing a pest by hand. Complete removal of infected plants can help prevent further spread of a disease. This involves taking the diseased plant *completely* out of the garden area, not just pulling it and leaving it in the area.

TIP: The cannabis plant is susceptible to tobacco mosaic virus, so ban smoking or chewing tobacco products from the garden area to prevent contamination.

BIOLOGICAL CONTROL

Biological control relies on naturally occurring organisms. In some instances this may be a fungus or bacterium that attacks the pest when environmental conditions are right. It can also refer to the action of beneficial insects.

Monitoring strips are a good way to stay ahead of infestations.

CHEMICAL CONTROL

If a pest population reaches threshold levels (damage above what you're willing to tolerate) despite preventive measures and other types of controls, you can use chemical insecticides as a last resort. Even chemicals are not a foolproof way of controlling pests. If the pest is too far along in its growth cycle or has built up a resistance to a pesticide, then use of a chemical might do more harm than good.

Chemicals for insect control are divided into several classes: conventional synthetic pesticides, inorganic insecticides, botanical insecticides, microbial insecticides, smothering agents, and synthetic insecticides derived from microbes.

Toxicity of a pesticide to humans and other mammals can be high (for products such as carbaryl) or low (for products such as pyrethrins) or anywhere in between. Botanical and microbial pesticides tend to break down more rapidly than conventional pesticides. Rapid breakdown can be favorable because the insecticide is in the environment for a shorter period of time, but it also offers a shorter period of protection for the plant, which can result in the need for more frequent applications.

Insecticidal soaps and oils are often considered part of an organic pest control program. Oils work on the basis of suffocation of insects and their eggs. Soaps are used as desiccants to dry out soft-bodied insects. Both need to come into direct contact with the insect to be effective. Take care when using these products to avoid damage to cannabis leaves. Plants are more sensitive to soaps and oils when they are under stress from high temperatures (less than 85°F).

When using pesticides, *always* follow the directions on the label. Do not apply at higher rates than directed on the label. Most insecticides have a preharvest limitation, which means the product is not allowed if the crop is going to be harvested within a certain number of days. For most of the newer insecticides, this limitation is just 1 day or even 0 days, but for most of the harsher insecticides, the limit can range from 3 to 45 days. Be certain to wear protective clothing if the label suggests it; wearing waterproof gloves and a long-sleeved shirt is always a good idea anyway.

Pesticides are available at local garden centers and via online ordering.

COMMON PESTS

Common sucking pests that attack cannabis cultivated indoors include spider mites, aphids, and, in rare instances, whiteflies. Aphids and most sucking insects can be controlled through the process of spraying a low-impact insecticide such as neem or a pyrethrin-based insecticide (with latex gloves on) and then manually smashing all visible eggs and live pests. Note that spider mites are arachnids and are more resistant to some pesticides. You can rotate three pesticides to get more control over them.

Aphids

Identification: Aphids are small (1/16 to 1/8-inch long), soft-bodied insects commonly called plant lice. Virtually every plant has at least one aphid species that attacks it. These small insects are masters of reproduction and are often found in great numbers on stems or leaves. Some species even feed on the roots of plants. They range in color from green to brown, red, black, or purple. Some species may even have different color forms in the same colony. Most have their soft exoskeleton exposed, but some species produce waxy, cottony strands that cover the body. These are often called woolly aphids.

Aphids are identified by their sucking mouthparts; long, thin legs; long antennae; pear-shaped body; and pair of tube-like structures (called cornicles) arising from the posterior of the abdomen. A magnifying glass may be needed to see the short cornicles of some species. These cornicles are the ducts of glands that produce alarm odors. Aphids may be winged or wingless, and colonies often have both forms.

Aphids excrete a sugary liquid called *honeydew*. This honeydew drips onto plant foliage or other structures and provides a suitable environment for black sooty molds to grow. Ants often tend or care for aphids in return for the honeydew. Therefore, if ants are running over a plant, look carefully for aphids.

Types of Damage: Each plant reacts differently to aphid attacks. Some plants show no response to the aphids, while others produce distorted (twisted, curled, or swollen) leaves or stems. Occasionally, aphids may actually kill leaves or small shoots. Since aphids may move from one plant to another, they may transmit plant diseases from their contaminated sucking mouthparts. The important thing to remember about aphids is that they are *tremendous* repro-ducers, and, with their ability to fly, they tend to constantly re-infest plants.

Control: Outdoors, aphids usually only cause aesthetic damage. Indoors, aphids can be a more serious issue. The old name "plant lice" is appropriate for the way the aphid can reproduce indoors. Manual removal and/or spraying pyrethrin-based insecticide is usually sufficient to control aphids aboveground. When encountering actual aphid species that are subterranean, use imidaclo-prid, a synthetic nicotine, to control them. *Do not waste time* when treating aphids that are prolific breeders. With persistent species of root aphids, rotate azadirachtin, imidacloprid, and spinosad in a 4 to 7 day rotation. Dipping the plants in a bucket of pesticide solution may be more economical and a better delivery method than a root drench in some instances.

Fungus Gnats

Fungus gnats are small flies. The larvae of many species live in moist soil, fungi, or decaying vegetation. Some can be found in the soil of potted or outdoor plants. Adults are a nuisance when they emerge and fly around within the home environment; larvae are rarely seen but some species can damage plant seedlings by feeding on the roots.

Identification: Adults are small (2.5 to 3.2 millimeters) gray or black insects that resemble mosquitoes with long slim legs and thread-like antennae. They have one pair of wings that are clear or light gray with a diagnostic Y-shaped vein in the wing. The larvae are 5.5-millimeter-long maggots with black shiny heads and a legless white to clear body.

Fungus gnats take a few weeks to really grow their numbers. Use monitoring strips.

Life cycle: The fungus gnat goes through complete metamorphosis that includes egg, larva, pupa, and adult stages. A life cycle can be completed in 3 to 4 weeks. Females lay between fifty to three hundred eggs that will hatch in 4 to 7 days at room temperature (70°F to 75°F). At a temperature of 72°F, larvae feed for 2 weeks. Pupation happens in the medium and takes 5 to 6 days before adults emerge. Adults live for about a week, mate, and start the process over again. Many generations can be present at the same time throughout the year.

Feeding adults, while annoying, feed on water and plant nectar and pose no harm to humans. Larvae feed in the soil on decaying plant matter, fungi, and plant roots. Larval feeding can stunt plant growth, kill seedlings, and reduce overall plant growth. Both adults and larvae have the ability to spread plant pathogens that can, in turn, lead to plant death.

Control: Inspect plants and soil for adults during watering or place yellow sticky traps in pots. Check sticky traps every 2 to 3 days. Gently tap or shake the plant and adults will fly off, making them easier to find. Potato slices can be used to check for larvae. Peel and slice a raw potato into 1-inch pieces and place ⅜ inches deep in the growing medium. Larvae will move onto the potato slice to feed and can be easily counted. Check the potato a couple of times a week by picking up the slice and examining it for larvae.

Cultural control: Eliminating excess moisture is the most important control method. Fungus gnats do best in moist medium, so key management strategies include avoiding overwatering plants and making sure plants are well drained. The top surface of the medium should be allowed to dry before watering again. This helps to kill larvae and eliminate the next generation. Minimize organic matter, especially on the top surface of the plant, to reduce breeding sites. Note that diatomaceous earth placed on or in the medium does not control fungus gnat adults or larvae. It is important to keep gnats away from plants to prevent infestation; keeping doors and windows closed or screened is an easy way to accomplish this. Avoid introducing infested plants into an uninfected home or greenhouse to avoid infestation. Yellow sticky traps can act as a physical control method by trapping adults, preventing them from producing eggs and limiting future populations.

Biological control: Biological controls can be effective in the management of fungus gnats. There are two commercially available: *Steinernema* nematodes and *Hypoaspis* mites. *Steinernema* nematodes have a simple life cycle starting with juvenile nematodes seeking a host insect. The nematode enters a fungus gnat's body through the mouth, anus, or spiracles (holes through which an insect breathes). Once in the body, symbiotic bacteria are released from the nematode, which in turn kill the host insect. The dead insect and bacteria are food for the nematode until it reaches the adult stage, where it reproduces and starts the process again in the medium. Completion of its life cycle occurs in a few days. This nematode is not dangerous to humans or pets.

Hypoaspis are small (0.8 millimeters), tan mites that feed voraciously on gnat eggs and larvae. The life cycle of the mites is 13 days from egg to death. They will reproduce in the growing medium, so they'll stay around to feed for many generations. Reapplication can be made in 2 to 4 weeks, if needed, and complete control can be expected in 2 to 4 applications. Like *Steinernema*, these mites dwell in the medium and are not harmful to humans or pets.

Chemical control: Commercially available Bt products are very effective for reducing larval populations. *Bacillus thuringiensis* (Bt) subspecies *israelensis* (Bt/H-14) can be applied as a drench and will slowly kill larvae in the soil. Bt is a naturally occurring bacterial organism derived from soil (so, perhaps technically a bio-pesticide). It is applied as an organically approved pesticide that produces proteins toxic to an insect. The proteins halt the digestive system so the insect stops eating and starves to death. There are several different strains of Bt that are effective against a number of insects, including adults and larvae of some beetles, flies, and moths. However, only the *israelensis* subspecies is effective against fungus gnats. Reapplication can be made every other week, if needed, and complete control can be expected in 2 to 4 applications. Cedar oil sprayed on the surface of the medium can greatly reduce populations, providing control in 2 to 3 applications. You can use imidacloprid for severe infestations or quick control.

Spider Mites

Spider mites are not insects but are more closely related to spiders. These arachnids have four pairs of legs, no antennae, and a single, oval body region. Most spider mites have the ability to produce a fine silk webbing. Spider mites are very tiny, growing to less than $\frac{1}{50}$ of an inch (0.4 millimeters).

Spider mites have tiny mouthparts modified for piercing individual plant cells and removing the contents. This results in tiny yellow or white speckles. When many of these feeding spots occur near each other, the foliage takes on a yellow or bronzed cast. Once the foliage of a plant becomes bronzed, it often drops off prematurely. Heavily infested plants may be discolored, stunted, or even killed. Web-producing spider mites may coat the foliage with a fine silk that collects dust and looks dirty.

Life cycles: Spider mite species are either warm-weather or cool-weather pests (though they can come inside from the outdoors). The two-spotted, European red honey locust, and oak spider mites do best in dry, hot summer weather. The spruce and southern red spider mites do best in cool spring and fall weather.

All spider mites go through the same stages of development. Adult females usually lay eggs on their host plants. The eggs hatch in days to weeks into the first stage, called a larva. Larvae are round bodied and have only three pairs of legs. The larvae feed for a few days, seek a sheltered spot to rest, and then molt (shed their "skin") into the first nymphal stage. The first nymph now has four pairs of legs. The first nymphs feed a few days, rest, and molt into the second nymph. The second nymphs feed, rest, and molt into the adult stage. The males are usually the size of the second nymph and have pointed abdomens. The females have rounded abdomens and are the largest mites present.

TWO-SPOTTED SPIDER MITE

Most spider mites spend the winter in the egg stage, but the two-spotted spider mite overwinters as adult females resting in protected places. Two-spotted is the most common spider mite for cannabis. The two-spotted spider mite is an example of a "warm season" mite. This pest has been reported to affect more than 180 host plants including field crops, ornamental plants, houseplants, and weeds.

This is who is causing that stipling—a spider mite!

The females overwinter in the soil or on host plants. The females become active in April and May when they seek out the undersides of leaves on suitable hosts. Each female may lay more than a hundred eggs. A single generation may require as much as 20 to as few as 5 days, depending on the temperature. These mites prefer hot, dry weather and often do not reach damaging populations in

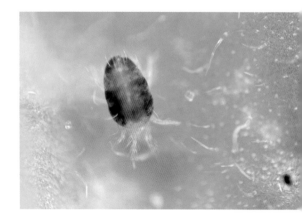

cool, rainy periods. In the summer, the adults and nymphs are white with two greenish spots. However, overwintering females usually turn reddish orange and can be mistaken for other mite species.

SPRUCE SPIDER MITE

The spruce spider mite is a common cool-season mite (and another pest that can invade the indoors from the outside). This pest can be found on all types of conifers, from spruces and pines to junipers and arborvitae. This mite spends the winter in the egg stage attached to host plants. The eggs hatch in March to April, and the mites can complete development in 3 to 4 weeks. If summer temperatures are constantly over 90°F, this mite lays eggs and becomes dormant. These eggs and adults resume activity in the fall when cooler temperatures return.

Control: Early detection of spider mites, before damage is noticed, is important. The tiny spider mites can be detected by taking a piece of white paper or cardboard and tapping some plant foliage over it. The mites can be seen walking slowly on the paper.

- **Cultural Control—Quarantine and Inspection**
  The two-spotted spider mite is often introduced on new plants. When purchasing new plants, carefully inspect the lower leaf surface for any signs of mite activity. New plants should be quarantined from other plants until you are sure that no mites are present.

- **Cultural Control—RemovE Infested Plants**

- **Biological Control—Predators**
  There are numerous insects (lacewings and lady beetles) that prey on spider mites. However, the most commonly sold predators are other types of mites. Predatory mites (usually *Phytoseiulus* spp., *Amblyseius* spp., or *Metaseiulus* spp.) can be purchased and released onto infested plants. Be sure to check the label to determine which species is appropriate. Some species are host specific, and each predator works better under different environmental conditions. If predators are used, do not apply pesticides that will kill them.

- **Chemical Control—"Soft Pesticides"**
  Most spider mites can be controlled with insecticidal oils and soaps. The oils, both horticultural oil and dormant oil, can be used. Remember that mites are very tiny and soaps and oils work by contact only. Therefore, thorough coverage of the plant is necessary for good control.

- **Chemical Control—Miticides**

  Spider mites are usually not killed by regular insecticides, so be sure to check the pesticide label to see if the word *miticide* is present. Pesticides claiming "for mite suppression" are usually weak miticides and will not perform well. There are few products available to the homeowner. Dicofol is registered for over-the-counter use but is difficult to find. Acephate, dimethoate, chlorpyrifos, disulfoton, and malathion have over-the-counter product labels but are considered weak miticides.

  Abemactin, Floramite, a pyrethroid, and manual removal may all be necessary to remove this persistent pest. Be mindful of final spray time and harvest. Rotate sprays every 4 to 7 days while manually removing pests.

  Unlikely to find their way indoors, members of the mantis family are commonly found on cannabis plants in the wild.

CHAPTER 10

Harvest and Ingestion

Now that you've read the book and you understand how to grow your own cannabis, you need to learn how to harvest, cure, and prepare it for ingestion.

Unlike many psychoactive substances, the cannabinoids are not toxic to humans. The amount of cannabis that you would theoretically need to consume to be a fatal dose is so large that no one can take it. However, cannabis can induce many different effects and side effects.

Desired effects of cannabis include:
- Distraction from pains (though cannabis cannot treat pain directly)
- Euphoria
- Altered state of mind
- Relaxed cardiovascular effects
- Muscle relaxation

Side effects of cannabis include:
- Increased appetite
- Inebriation
- Feelings of anxiety
- Paranoia
- Disorientation
- A mechanical effect on the memory recycling systems of the brain that causes memory loss symptoms
- R eddening of the eyes

Cannabis is often prescribed medically to counteract the wasting effects of chemotherapy and as an aid in treating multiple sclerosis, Parkinson's disease, neurological disorders, PTSD, chronic pain, and asthma and other respiratory issues. Migraine headaches, arthritis, and Crohn's disease may also be controlled by cannabis.

Some of the ingestion techniques have a tendency to produce predictable combinations of side effects. Chronic use must be self-monitored for symptoms of overconsumption such as chronic bronchitis, a strain on the respiratory system, lethargy, and even paranoia. In these instances, if you must consume cannabis, you should consider changing ingestion methods. In rare instances, allergies to constituents of the plant or horticultural residues can occur.

INGESTION METHODS
Smoking
- Inhaling the vapors produced from burning
- Dried flower
- Kief
- Hashish
- Traditional hash (hydrocarbon extractions)

Ingestion
- Pills
- Tinctures
- Foods

Before you can ingest, you have to harvest, cure, and prepare the product.

TIMING OF HARVEST
Commonly, cannabis plants are harvested based on the maturity of the capitate trichome. An astute grower has the opportunity to have one final hand in the effect of the cannabis when consumed.

The capitate trichome of the cannabis plant begins its final stages of maturation as a clear membrane containing a clear, oily liquid that contains the highest concentration of cannabinoids in the plant along with terpenes and other essential oils. You will experience a noticeably more stimulating effect that is often disorienting in a high dose if you harvest when this liquid is clear. Common side effects include elevated heart rate, confusion, and a sort of semi-creative restlessness. Retailers in legal markets have taken to describing cannabis with these types of effects as "sativa dominant" or daytime smoke. This is no doubt due to the longtime association between the narrow leaf drug plants and a slightly more hallucinogenic effect and a noticeable lack of a narcotic side effect.

CAPITATE TRICHOME

Clear Trichomes
Immature with mostly precursor cannabinoids

Cloudy Trichomes
At their peak with fully-realized THC

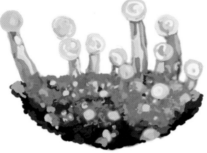

Amber Trichomes
Past their peak with degrading THC

As the capitate trichome matures, it transitions in appearance from clear to cloudy. During most production cycles, before the later-formed trichomes become cloudy, the earlier formed ones begin to take on an amber hue (or another color).

The most common time to harvest is when approximately half of the trichomes have taken on a colored hue. Professionals in legal markets who manage acquisitions are commonly trained to look for this when purchasing for medical outlets or retail operations. Harvesting at this stage ensures a respectable amount of flower development and a good representation of desirable effects as well as a wide range of possible side effects.

The second time to harvest is any time after the 50/50 clear/cloudy stage when more of the trichomes are cloudy. The third time to harvest is when all the trichomes are amber colored. These late harvests are characterized by richly colored capitate trichomes and sometimes an overdevelopment of the flowers characterized by opening of their calyxes. They have a noticeably more narcotic effect, leaving most people feeling sedentary after consumption. This is described as nighttime smoke by purveyors and associated with wide leaf drug plants or "indica dominant." Many lifelong cannabis users do not know that trichome maturity is a direct factor in marijuana's overall narcotic effect.

HOW TO HARVEST
Harvesting

Physically cutting down a marijuana plant *is* the harvest. Traditional harvesting used a scythe, which has long been the symbol of this process, and in that tradition you'd cut a plant's main stock and hang it if it is freestanding. However, staked plants usually must have their support structure removed before cutting the plant down. Oftentimes, when using trellising techniques, you can just cut out the flowers

Above: Removing as much leaf material as possible when first cut can improve aroma.

Top: This (Cannabis indica) crop is getting close to harvest.

and an extra 4 inches or so of the lower stem to allow you to hang the flower structure. If plants are ripening slowly, you always have an option of pulling (harvesting) only what is up to your standards and allowing the remainder to ripen (that is, leave it growing until it's more mature).

When trimming, cut away leaves from the flowers using comfortable scissors, or you can purchase a trimming machine because it's a lot of cutting. Large yields equal sore hands. The point of this is to remove the less potent leaf structures so the (mostly) stronger flower structures remain. It also promotes a better flavor profile for inhalation and looks better. From a production standpoint, it is a countermeasure against mold and fungus in this final stage.

Drying

Variations on harvest and drying cannabis are too numerous to be cataloged. I'll cover the method used by medical growers in the United States and competition champions from abroad, and touch on some variations.

You can purchase drying racks from hydroponic stores. Commercial growers sometimes use alternate techniques such as drying in paper sacks. These methods produce a slightly different final product. Hang drying in a closet is an easy, effective way to ensure a strong flower with a desirable appearance and aroma.

Currently, growers concerned with the quality of their final product in competitive markets hang their flowers to dry in the dark. Constructing a chamber or closet that operates at 75°F and 50 percent RH is the first step. Turning off the lights in your flowering chamber is another way to dry, but obviously you then can't use the space to grow plants while you're drying the harvest.

String clothing lines, fishing line, string, nylon cord, or twine across the chamber so that there's a place to hang the harvest. There are a lot of factors during the last week of the grow that can affect how long it takes for flowers to dry. Primarily, the more water there is inside the vascular structures of the plants when they are cut, the longer hang drying will take. Typical times range from 8 to 14 days.

Flowers are dry enough to cure when they contain approximately 12.5 percent moisture. Growers use a simple test to determine this: the main stem of the flower should snap when bent back on itself. If a stem doesn't offer resistance and break, then the flowers aren't dry yet.

DRYING CLOSET

Fan / heater

Cured product often has a lighter color and more complex aroma.

Curing

Curing is a process that accomplishes two objectives:
- It ages terpenes and flavonoides while activating some of the THC
- It draws the remaining moisture out of the flower

The moisture remaining in plants after drying is usually unpleasant in aroma and flavor. Curing can be done inexpensively and effectively in sealed Mason jars. Place the dried flowers in the jars so that they are half to three-quarters full. Close the jars for 4 hours. Flowers will be moist again at the end of this period as well as take on a slightly different aroma. Leave the container open for a 24-hour period and repeat this process, closing the jar for 4 additional hours every time and reducing the amount of open time by 4 hours. Repeat until flowers have reached the desired aroma.

CONSUMPTION METHODS

There are different ways to consume marijuana. The two most common are smoking or inhaling vapors and eating the product.

Smoking

Smoking is the process of inhaling the vapors produced from burning marijuana. This has been historically documented as far back as the Sumerian tribes. There is evidence that's been discovered of the tribes burning plants in a tent or open bonfire. Smoking remains the most common ingestion technique.

Consuming Dried Flowers

This is the most commonly consumed form of cannabis and is the base for most of the following preparations. Dried flowers contain the highest concentrations of active and inactive ingredients in a cannabis plant.

Kief

Kief is a mix of terpines and capitate trichomes that resembles powder or sand. Dry or wet sieving 45- to 120-micron-sized terpines and trichomes yields this product, which can be smoked or used in further preparations. Typically, cannabis is chilled with ice if it's wet sieved and with dry ice if you're using dry sieving. Separating the water-based plant material from the oil-based pubescent structures increases the potency of cannabinoids and secondary chemicals by discarding the less potent plant material.

Hashish

The current definition of hashish or hash is a smokable preparation either of processed kief or a hydrocarbon extract. Pressed kief is the simplest. Heating kief activates a portion of the THC, so heating and pressing ruptures membranes, releasing oils while activating cannabinoids (mainly THC). This is the traditional hash.

The goal is to grow as much of these structures on flowers as possible.

Water or bubble hash is a wet ice water sieving of kief. It produces a slightly different product than dry sieving kief. The ice water helps to separate the oil- and water-based parts of the plant in a way that produces a high-quality product in the low-micron filters or bags and a slightly lower quality product in the 90- to 120-micron range.

Traditional Hash
HYDROCARBON EXTRACTIONS

Resurging in popularity, hydrocarbon extractions of oil-based cannabinoids can be consumed on flower, meaning the oil-based cannabinoid is placed on dried flowers and then burned and inhaled. So, you load a bowl, drip oil on the dried flowers in the bowl, light, and inhale.

Extractions can be burned and inhaled without flowers by using a heated nail or skillet or a vaporizer with a cartomizer. When a hydrocarbon source such as butane or alcohol comes in contact with dried cannabis, it begins to pull oil-based compounds out and away from water-based plant material. This is essentially how all oils, shatters, and waxes are made.

Oils: Oils are the more viscous extractions or uncleaned butane hash oil (BHO, also called butane honey oil). It's traditionally simply called "honey oil" and it is the precursor for shatter wax and so forth.

Shatters: If you look at the modern concentrate consistencies, the shatters are the next step in room temperature stability after oils but before waxes. Shatters are the BHO that is purged in a vacuum on low heat for 2 to 4 hours. Purging a winterized extraction with heat produces an opaque product that looks yellow to amber-red in color. A good shatter breaks like glass upon impact after 10 to 30 minutes in a freezer—hence its name.

Waxes: Vacuuming with low heat for more than 4 hours continues to change the consistency to something that can resemble hard peanut butter or a thin sugar cookie. (Note that the word *vacuuming* means placing the BHO in a Decatur oven or a similar homemade device; it's also called "purging" and, more recently, "pulling.") The concentrate loses its opaqueness and becomes yellow to gray in color, but it is usually very stable. Prolonged exposure to low heat and vacuuming can change flavor profiles and even evaporate some minor chemical constituents. The common range of time required is 10 to 32 hours, with 10 to 12 being the norm, and longer if a large amount of plant lipids and waxes remain.

After sufficient exposure, the hydrocarbon, referred to by cooks as the solvent, is then evaporated in a Pyrex dish or in a catch basin in an extraction machine. Buying an extraction machine is not necessarily financially feasible for most home producers; many extraction machines now are devices into which you place a Pyrex dish. Purging through heat, vacuuming with heat, or combining solvents to make a sort of polar slurry with decreasingly dangerous hydrocarbons that have higher boiling points are the three current methods of purging.

These different processes control the consistency and flavor of the final product.

- Long, slow heat purging can produce a crystalline texture that returns to a melted sugar consistency when it's heated.
- Fast heat purging produces an oily consistency.

Vaporizers are a discreet way to ingest concentrates.

- Vacuum purging (also known as "vacuuming") with heat for 2 to 4 hours usually produces a tackier, taffy-like consistency dubbed *shatter* because after time or when it's chilled, it breaks like hard plastic or glass.

Further vacuum purging with heat produces the more stable forms of concentrate called *wax*. The concentrate will take on a porous appearance due to trapped pockets of hydrocarbon escaping as gas from the concentrate. It can range from a yellow color with a consistency that resembles chewed gum to a gray that looks like lava rock but breaks down quickly with pressure or heat.

These products still contain the lipids and waxes of the cannabis plant that, as time passes, are being looked at more and more as contaminates. The mixing of solvents with different boiling points and polarity have led to chilling processes where the lipids and waxes can be frozen and filtered out before evaporation. These polar shatters vary widely in color and texture based on hydrocarbons and material used.

The evaporation process is all that's needed for the purge. Mix butane with a product that's 91 percent alcohol and 9 percent water; an example is to mix the butane with isopropyl alcohol that's 91 percent alcohol (the other 9 percent of the solution is water). The butane boils off well before the alcohol, which is followed by the water. It is easy to test for cleanliness purity with a hot nail because the product tastes awful if alcohol is present and sizzles if water is present. If it sizzles but tastes good, the water is still there. No sizzle means there's no water left. If the product tastes good and does not sizzle, the water has been eliminated because water boils off after alcohol, which burns off after butane. For higher concentrations of alcohol like 99 percent, add water to the slurry. (The common proportion is to add 2 to 4 tablespoons water. Higher concentration

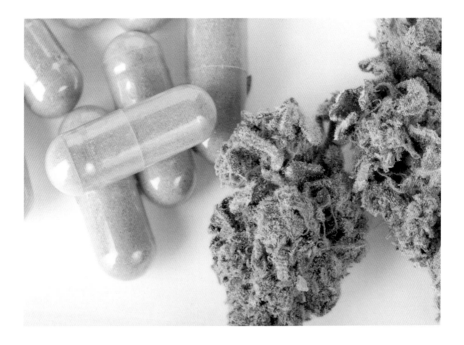

Pills are one way to control dosages with edibles.

of alcohol is not ideal, but some people use it so you must add a little water to facilitate the purging without leaving solvents or burning your product.)

Quick-wash techniques are also used to make alcohol-only oils. Typically, cannabis is super chilled with dry ice or left in a freezer overnight and washed with alcohol for 45 seconds or so; then, the alcohol containing the extract is filtered into a Pyrex dish. The alcohol is evaporated using heat and tested as discussed.

Combinations of oils and dry or wet sieved kief that are heated and pressed are referred to as *jelly hashes*. For the entire 1990s, this hybrid of traditional and modern technique produced a highly active, smokable product that was consumed in conjunction with flowers, independently, or even eaten by the brave seeking the most psychoactively hallucinogenic effect available.

INGESTION METHODS

Eating cannabis has been a popular ingestion technique for centuries. The heart of it is ingestion of an activated form of THC that can be easily absorbed into the bloodstream while in the stomach. Dried flower contains only low levels of activated THC and is not practical for consumption if a euphoric effect is desired. Heat and an assisting molecule such as lecithin in milk or coconut oil are used to facilitate absorption into the bloodstream. This activates the THC and bonds it with the carrier so it can be absorbed in sufficient amounts in the bloodstream. Cookies and brownies are the traditional edibles, using butter as a carrier. The variety of products available in legal markets is staggering, and cannabis-infused butter is readily available to make almost anything edible.

Pills

Generally, pills are thicker concentrations of cannabis carried by coconut oil or glycerin packed into a pill at a measured amount for ease of use and help monitoring dosages.

To make a pill, take some of the concentrate and place in a Pyrex dish. Then add some coconut oil or glycerin. Using low heat, mix well to combine the substances. Allow the mixture to cool slightly, then fill the capsules. What you're doing is activating the THC and providing a carrier to aid the digestion of plant extracts.

Though it doesn't matter which solvent you use, or which consistency it is, you should remember that actually eating a concentrate containing high solvent levels in it can have negative side effects; the consumption of butane through the ingestion symptom is *not* what you're shooting for, so the closer to a pure product, the better.

Tinctures

Tinctures are liquid preparations using alcohol or glycerin as a carrier to assist absorption into the bloodstream. They are typically sprayed into the mouth or under the tongue for a fast delivery method. They are made in the same fashion as pills but with more alcohol or glycerin so it is liquidy/viscous for delivery drops or sprays.

Foods

With this knowledge of harvesting and curing, you will be able to experiment adding cannabis (ground or extractions) to food also. Just like regular cooking, there are thousands, maybe millions, of recipes. These myriad recipes can be found on numerous websites. Or, the best thing to do is to experiment using it. But here's one popular way to ingest cannabis in the form of butter (which can also be used in baked goods).

Cannabis Butter

¼ ounce finely ground cannabis buds
½ cup (1 stick) salted butter

Melt the butter slowly over low heat. Add the ground buds, a little at a time, stirring after each addition. Simmer over very low heat, about 45 minutes. Strain out the buds, leaving the infused melted butter in a storage dish. Refrigerate.

Glossary

Air pump—the device used to move air into reservoir

Air stone—a fitting on the end of the air pump hose that goes into the reservoir and defuses air entering the reservoir

Anion—a negatively charged ion or group of ions

Auxin—one of the five plant hormones; controls many growth functions and characteristics such as lateral branching and root growth

Axillary bud—an embryonic shoot that lies at the junction of the stem and petiole of the plant

Base grow formula—your base is the main fertilizer you start creating your nutrient solution from; it composes the majority of your solution; additives and supplements are added after base; traditional garden fertilizing is usually only a base fertilizer; complete or incomplete fertilizers can be considered base if they are your main ingredient and everything is added to it

Burn—a catchall term to describe the damage caused by heat or over-fertilization

Calyx—the whirls of sepals on a flower containing essential oils or protecting a seed

Cannabinoid receptors—concentrated in certain areas of the brain associated with thinking, memory, pleasure, coordination, and time perception; there are also cannabinoid receptors on nerves in other parts of the body

Capitate trichome—a resin-producing glandular structure on a pubescent stalk; located in the highest concentration on mature flower structures

Cation—an ion or group of ions that are charged positively

Chiller—a device that uses a radiator-like manifold and cold water to cool air

Corolla—all of the petals of a flower collectively

Cotyledon—the first upper structures of a seedling; contained in the seed, they are oval with rounded margins

EC—electrical conductivity

Emitter—the fitting where water leaves the irrigation system

Endosperm—the nutrient cache of a seed

Exhaust—moves air out of a space

Fallout nutrients—nutrients hardening into crystal globs, or chunks in your reservoir sinking to the bottom and becoming unavailable

Foliar spray—a solution sprayed on the leaves of a plant

Gibberellin—the hormone associated with intermodal spacing and other growth structures

High-pressure sodium (HPS)—a type of bulb that contains sodium under high pressure to produce a fall-like spectrum of light

Hood—the upper portion of a lamp assembly; the outside protects the bulb and the inside is usually reflective

Intake—moves air into a space

Internode—the area of stem in between nodes

Low-pressure sodium lights—similar to HPS but under low pressure

Lumens—a measurement of light; 1 candle at 1 square foot

Macronutrients—group of mineral elements that plants primarily consume: nitrogen, potassium, etc.

Mercury vapor—a bulb containing mercury vapor

Metal halide (MH)—a halide bulb with a metal filament that produces a bluer summer spectrum

Micronutrients—the elements plants generally need smaller concentrations of

Mother plant—technically any plant you take a clone from; typically one or more plants will be grown in vegetation for this express purpose, yielding more clones each time

Node—the point on a stem where two or more leaves emerge

Nutrient sinks—located primarily in the petioles; they store sugar and simple constituents the plant uses to facilitate growth processes and mitigate stress

Nutrient solution—water with nutrients in it

Nutrients—mineral elements or molecular chains used to facilitate plant processes after uptake

Organic—products complying with state or OMRI manufacturing criteria

Petal—any of the separate parts of the corolla of a flower

pH—potential hydrogen

Photoperiod—the measure of light cycle; that is, how much light or dark a plant lives in

Photosynthesis—the complex process by which carbon dioxide, water, and certain inorganic salts are converted into carbohydrates by green plants, algae, and certain bacteria

Photosynthetically active radiation (PAR)—the radioactive energy used by plants in the photosynthetic process

Polar slurry— A mixture of alcohol, butane,and concentrated plant extract. The slurry becomes "polar" when alcohol is added to the mix.

Polytube—flexible plastic irrigation tubing

PPM—parts per million

Propagation—the cloning or seeding of plants

PVC—the material commonly used in household plumbing

Quick-release system (CO_2)—a tank and regulator that releases measured amounts of CO_2

Radicle—the pointy small root that emerges from a seed; the first part of a seedling to emerge

Relative humidity—a measurement of how much moisture is in the air at a specific temperature

Reservoir—the container filled with the nutrient solution

Rock wool sleeve—a plastic wrapper or bag wrapped around rock wool; often used in or in place of gutters by merely cutting out planting sites and poking holes for drainage

Scarification—roughing the seed to allow moisture to permeate

Seed coat—the outer layer of the seed

Sepal—one of the individual leaves or parts of a calyx

Spaghetti tube—a small irrigation tube

Stake and dripper—an assembly that fits on spaghetti tube to drip water onto plants; the stake holds the assembly in place usually by being inserted into the medium

Stipule—the small outgrowth at the base of a leaf

Stomata—the "mouth organs" on the undersides of leaves

Synthetic—products not in compliance with organic standards; usually containing refined ingredients

Tepid range—60°F–80°F

THC or tetrahydrocannabinol—the chemical responsible for most of marijuana's psychological effects; THC changes behavior by binding—fitting together like a lock and key—to receptors on nerve cells, which then respond with a change in activity

Total dissolved salts (TDS)—the amount of dissolved salt in a solution

True leaves—the first leaves to form with the plant's normal characteristics

Water soluble—basically a solution that is water and salt; water soluble means something will break down in the water, forming a solution

Photo Credits

Photos appearing on pages 6, 10, 11, 12, 13, 14, 15, 17, 19, 20, 23, 24, 25, 37, 38, 41 (bottom), 46, 50, 51, 52, 53, 56, 57, 61, 96, 97, 115, 122, 152, 161, 162, 165, 167, 168, 171, 174, 178, 180, 181, 183, and 184 courtesy of Shutterstock.com.

Photos appearing on pages 31 and 41 (top) courtesy Cool Springs Press archive.

Illustrations appearing on pages 9, 18, 21, 27, 29, 34, 48, 54, 55, 100, 116, 119, 124, 125, 126, 128, 130, 131, 132, 133, 134, 135, 156, 157, 177, and 179 courtesy of Shannon Rahkola.

Photos appearing on pages 42 (top and bottom), 43, 58, 59, and 123 courtesy of Joshua Sheets.

Index

Meet Joshua Sheets

Joshua Sheets began gardening with his grandfather at the age of six on the grandfather's 3-acre Victory-style garden. Joshua's first job was landscaping for the archdioces of Seattle, and then he ran several conventional gardens and started a successful production facility for annuals. Eventually, his passion for controlled environmental agriculture led to running multiple gardens, both indoor and outdoor.

In his early life, Sheets served several months in prison for manufacturing marijuana, which at that time was illegal in Washington State. He eventually earned his way to a minimum-security facility, where he worked for the Department of Natural Resources as a firefighter and reforester. Sheets then graduated from Peninsula College after earning a horticulture degree with presidential honors. His university experience led to an offer as an assistant college instructor where he wrote the teaching manual, *An Introductory Guide to Hydroponics and Indoor Gardening*, to bridge the gaps in the official syllabus for the hydroponic gardening curriculum. Sheets tested and refined his techniques for several years in this academic environment. He currently consults in the Seattle area for gardeners interested in setting up systems to grow hydroponically. Josh lives in Tumwater, Washington. This is his first book.